The Trifecta in Voting Barrier Causation

Voting, Elections, and the Political Process

Series Editors: Shauna Reilly and Stacy Ulbig

Receptive to studies in the American and comparative settings, the Voting, Elections, and the Political Process series examines the broadly defined electoral process. The series seeks scholarly monographs and edited volumes that investigate the ways in which voters, candidates, elected officials, parties, interest groups, the media, and others interact in the context of electoral politics. Works with a focus on individual attitudes and behavior, institutional and contextual influences, and the legal aspects of the electoral process are welcome. This series accepts interdisciplinary work using a variety of methodological approaches.

Recent Titles

The Trifecta in Voting Barrier Causation

Economics, Politics, and Race

Shauna Reilly

LEXINGTON BOOKS
Lanham • Boulder • New York • London

Published by Lexington Books
An imprint of The Rowman & Littlefield Publishing Group, Inc.
4501 Forbes Boulevard, Suite 200, Lanham, Maryland 20706
www.rowman.com

6 Tinworth Street, London SE11 5AL, United Kingdom

British Library Cataloguing in Publication Information Available

Library of Congress Control Number: 2020930622

ISBN 978-1-4985-8899-7 (cloth)
ISBN 978-1-4985-8901-7 (pbk)
ISBN 978-1-4985-8900-0 (electronic)

Contents

List of Figures and Tables

FIGURES

TABLES

Acknowledgments

Several students worked on this project during its inception and in its completion—we are very grateful for their assistance. Jessica Caudill Huff and I started the conversation and had the opportunity to examine some early results in a conference presentation. Samantha Davis did some preliminary data collection at the very start of the analysis. Hunter Howard also created a map to be used in chapter 1. I would also like to acknowledge and thank my contributors. Devon Moffett walked into a very difficult situation and learned very quickly that academic publishing is not easy, nor pretty. Devon had the ability to review many of the issues and determine several solutions to problems. There is not enough appreciation for the work he did on this project! I would like to acknowledge Ryan Yonk for his contributions to the theoretical development. I would also like to thank Jim Fiorelli for his valuable insights into the manuscript and his marvelous offer to assist in editing this beast—the over 900 comments were greatly appreciated! I must also recognize NKU's College of Arts and Sciences and Department of Political Science, Criminal Justice and Organizational Leadership for their assistance with travel funding to present chapters of this manuscript at conferences. Finally, I am sometime inept to recognizing the value of family, friends, and colleagues on their contributions to my research—for them I am extraordinarily grateful! This book is better for all of the contributions, big and small, that lead to its publication.

Chapter 1

A Fiscal Conservative Walks into a Race and Ethnicity Book

When I first imagined this book, I thought the post-2008 voting restrictions had to be more complex than the simple explanation of racism. After all, this is post-election of Obama America where there was an economic recession and increased polarization. Thus, began the exploration of different fiscal activities that contribute to the recession and consequentially their impacts on the voting restrictions. Economics—in terms of both fiscal cuts and economic threat—just seemed to be the explanation that no one was talking about and seemingly was a critical issue missing in the literature. I suggest that not only was economics a factor in reducing voter access but also in providing cover for less tasteful reasons for making it more difficult to vote for minority and poor voters. Our results show credence to the latter argument by showing that it is not *only* the economy, stupid! Rather that the book took a rightful turn toward looking at race and partisanship as well.[1] As the 2016 and 2018 elections demonstrate, partisanship and fiscal conservatism have had their impacts but one cannot discount the role that race plays in the decisions to narrowly define and restrict ballot access. Thus, the creation of the trifecta of causality—fiscal conservatism, partisanship, and racism—that leads to the decrease in voting accessibility post-2008.

As a fiscal conservative, it seems logical that there would be an attenuation of government (even election activities) when facing economic strife (like the 2008 recession) felt like a story that needs to be added in the voting literature. The external threat of shrinking budgets and economic rhetoric that created a threat from immigration on jobs and financial security not only for governments but also for voters. As financial limitations effect government expenditures, revenue, and even policy, it is reasonable that those cuts would also be felt in elections spending. Furthermore, one would expect that inexpensive options like online voter registration would increase in these instances. The

1

data demonstrates support for this idea. However, I was appalled, shocked and awed by the racial overtones that overtook the research on this issue. Seemingly, economic circumstances became part of the bootleggers and Baptists theory where under the cover of fiscal restraint we see partisan and racist motivations (Yandle 1983).

The rhetoric around 2016 illustrates that there were threats (economic, partisan, and racial) that have translated into hate and even discord in governing that had developed during the previous eight years. We are not post-racial; rather, we have become a society that is deeply immersed in the impacts of race and feel threatened when faced with changes to perceived social order (social order on an economic, partisan, and racial level). Thus, I posit a theory invoking threat as driving the changes to voting laws post-2008. These threats come in many forms—economic recessions that hurt state and personal fiscal status, partisan fear mongering, and a growing minority population—combining to create a perfect storm of creating an out-group to blame for perceived changes in social structure. These threats provide cover for one another as politicians pursued voting restrictions across the states.

Thus, a relatively fiscal conservative political scientist walked into a race and ethnicity politics book. How I walked out might shock you.

2018 ELECTION—WHAT WE KNOW NOW!

The impetus for this book came from the rhetoric around the 2016 election, where there was clearly a missing piece in voting rights suppression from the perspective of fiscal conservatism. There were substantial changes to voting rights laws post-2008 that coincided with many fiscal challenges facing our economy. Our country had experienced a recession and there were definitely repercussions felt from the *Shelby v. Holder* case on election laws, as such there appeared to be a window for new budget cuts where election laws were open to examination under the guise of fiscal responsibility. What if the voting restrictions were not a function of a deep-seated desire to suppress votes? Rather an unintended consequence of state budget cutting where the focus was on government expenditures but the consequence was voter suppression. However, the 2018 election, promising to be less controversial than 2016, demonstrated all of the themes in this book and amplified the arguments that it is not just a function of fiscal conservatism or partisanship or race but also a function of how these interact and find cover together.

So why do I suggest there is a role for economic threat in determining election activities? Certainly political behavior teaches us the role that economics plays on vote choice. Voters' interests are often tied to economics. Perception of the economy is almost as important as the actual state of the economy when it comes to vote choice. Local conditions predict evaluations of national economy (Hansford and Gomez 2015). Furthermore, economic factors influence vote as well as evaluate parties (Fair 1988). Voters hold candidates (particularly incumbents) accountable for the economy—more so for congressional and presidential incumbents than their subnational counterparts (Stein 1990). For example, looking at the Tax Cut and Jobs Act of 2017 (TCJA) every evaluation of the bill was from a partisan viewpoint—no one looked at it from a strictly economics perspective. National economic conditions influence outcomes of presidential elections (Nadeau and Lewis-Beck 2001); so it would not be a stretch to suggest that they influence the administration of those elections as well. Pointing to the role that the 2008–2009 recession had on states, unquestionably the recession had political and financial implications that were often expressed through hyperbole. Furthermore, even short-term fluctuations in economics affect presidential choice as well as public opinion of the presidency (Kinder and Kiewiet 1981). Yet, how does this transcend to electoral activities—such as spending?

Government revenue structure plays a significant role in its ability to provide services and answer the call for new policy. My other research focuses on direct democracy elections. A great example of the role that fiscal politics played in 2018 is to look at the thirty-eight ballot measures that involved the fiscal health of state and local governments. Economics can play a substantial role in electoral activity. We have seen that elections can change the course of state budgets (see California's Proposition 13 in 1977) but also are a costly activity for the state and local governments—both the "simple" administration of presidential election and the frequency of elections at the state and local level, length of ballot and even court challenges to electoral laws make for expensive affairs.

As such, electoral administration is not an inexpensive endeavor. Not only are states responsible for the majority of election expenses, there is a growing expectation about what the state will do to monitor elections. The aftermath of the presidential election in 2000 saw an increase in state oversight in the area of ballot format, changes to registration, voting technology, and voter education—all of which came at increased costs. Thus, the cost of elections plays a critical role in the number of services provided to voters and as such when there is a recession all services are on the cutting board (well those that do not explicitly violate laws).

The role of fiscal conservatism in decision-making and understanding the role of fiscal conservatism in the 2018 election provide context to our larger argument. Unsurprisingly, voters who do not approve of President Trump personally, continue to support the Republican Party on fiscal and moral issues. In fact, we know that public budgets were not a mobilizing force in the 2018 election (Arnosti and Pagano 2018). However, across the country, Republican voters continued to support candidates that urged fiscal restraint and sought to ensure that the costs of key government services did not rise. Across the country, local governments and state legislatures have raised concerns about the potential costs of increased voting hours. Concern about costs from local governments has focused primarily on the unfounded reality that most increased voting hours policies have fiscal impacts. They worry that the fiscal costs will result in other, potentially more important or popular policies being diminished through the increased costs. In 2016, 47 million Americans voted early (Stewart 2018). Both Massachusetts and Wisconsin have seen particularly vocal concern from local officials about mandates for expanded voting hours because of the added cost to the state (Lee 2018; Anderson 2018). In fact, in Madison County, Tennessee, the argument for not expanding early voting hours simply rested on not having the budget to pay employees to work extra hours (Friedman 2019). A 2019 bill passed in New York suggests that early voting will cost $7 million statewide. But, savings are expected by consolidating counties. At the county level, early voting is expected to cost between $500,000 and $1 million per county, many of which cannot afford these new costs (Silberstein 2019). Alabama secretary of state John Merrill argued that early voting is a waste of money and opens the door to electoral fraud (Howell 2019). Thus, states and local governments are making the case that the expense of elections means that activities such as early voting should be curtailed. While there are no studies demonstrating that early voting leads to increased voter fraud, it is an often-utilized argument.

Foremost in people's mind has been the role of partisanship in the voting restrictions. Seemingly, changes in voting rules (much like Jim Crow laws) continue to empower the party in government. The expected "blue wave" to carry Democrats to the majority in at least the house, and possibly the Senate (Baird 2018; Drucker 2018), was expected to reflect the growing discontent with policy changes implement by the Trump Administration. Of the Republicans who turned out to vote, 94 percent voted for Republican house candidates (Gawthrope 2018). Partisanship clearly wins over any viewpoints of presidential leadership. Further, news sources such as 538 (Silver 2018) suggested that the 2018 elections were highly predictable based on partisanship and not any more complicated than that.

Finally, in the exploration of the role of race on election administration, there were numerous occasions when race and immigration were at the forefront of the discussion in recent elections. In Georgia during the 2018 gubernatorial primary race, Michael Williams, a Republican candidate, proffered the Deportation Bus as the solution to Georgia's problems (Donnelly 2018), thus suggesting that immigrants (particularly illegal or undocumented immigrants) were the source of all problems in Georgia. In Mississippi, Republican senator Cindy Hyde-Smith indicated that she would be in front row if one of her supports invited her to a public hanging (Bradner 2018). She also went on to support voter suppression tactics that targeted voters from liberal college campuses (Bradner 2018). While these two issues were not necessarily connected from the outset, the suggestion of supporting lynching and voter suppression of liberals indicates clear connections of race and partisanship that permeated the election of 2018. Further, a radio ad run by a political action committee suggested that if Democrats were to win in Arkansas "white Democrats will be lynching Black folk again" (Demillo 2018)—again invoking racial imagery. There was also the never-ending discussion of the migrant caravan in the prelude to the 2018 election that was heading toward the US/Mexico border that threatened America. A Tennessee candidate (Marsh Blackburn) followed with an attack ad suggesting that the migrant group was full of "gang members . . . known criminals . . . people from the Middle East . . . possibly terrorists" adding fuel to an already rising flame of nativism (The Guardian 2018). These are just a drop[2] of the issues and stories about race that were covered in the 2018 election media coverage and demonstrating covert, and even overt, racism.

UNDERSTANDING VOTER ACCESS RESTRICTIONS

As we seek to understand what drives voter access restrictions and the how and why decisions are made to implement policy that limits that access, a solid understanding of both the history of voting restrictions and the most common policy instruments that are used to increase or decrease access to the ballot box is necessary. To situate our understanding of the changes that have taken place since 2008 (including voter identification laws, changes in early voting, absentee, and online registration), it is important to situate this work in the history of the Voting Rights Act (VRA). Regardless of the era, it is my belief that the motivations for limiting voter access are largely the same, and understanding those barriers leads to a better understanding of the implications of those restrictions on policy outcomes and Democratic and electoral processes involved.

WHY NOW? A BRIEF HISTORY OF
THE VOTING RIGHTS ACT

The recent restrictions of voting rights harkens back to the concerns and need for the original VRA in 1965. The VRA is one of the most important pieces of legislation ever passed. The VRA codified the Fifteenth Amendment by guaranteeing the right to vote regardless of race. This law was necessary to overcome many of the Jim Crow laws enacted in the post-Civil War South to prevent African Americans from voting. When the VRA was enacted, only one-third of voting-age African Americans were registered to vote despite two-thirds of whites being registered (Department of Justice—Federal Voting Rights). There were a number of citizen groups (outside of the government) who resisted the extension of the franchise to black voters (e.g., the Ku Klux Klan). These groups used intimidation at the polls, physical attacks, and even legal maneuvers to continue disenfranchisement of these voters. The courts dealt with a number of cases that attempted to limit disenfranchisement prior to the VRA (e.g., *Guinn v. United States* 1915; *Smith v. Allwright* 1944; *Gomillion v. Lightfood* 1960; *Baker v. Carr* 1962; *Reynolds v. Sims* 1964; *Wesberry v. Sanders* 1964) but failed to make inroads in changing the voting laws until the enactment of the VRA in 1965 (Department of Justice—Federal Voting Rights). After the passage of the VRA, federal employees were sent into the South to register black voters.

The VRA was further expanded and reauthorized in 1975, 1982, and 2006 to protect voting rights in other instances: protection of Latino voters, minority language voters, and racial gerrymandering. In 1975, the VRA was expanded to include other minority groups—interest groups for Latino, Asian American, Native Alaskan, and Native American groups focused on the discriminatorily nature of only providing English ballots in areas where English was not the dominant language. There was significant discussion of the cost of the 1975 expansion, which connects to the larger argument of this book. There was quite a bit of discussion of the increase in costs associated with publishing bilingual ballots during the congressional debate of this amendment. To provide some examples of these issues—in 1980 dollars, California reported spending $1.2 million for bilingual ballot printing; specifically, in San Francisco, the cost of printing Chinese-language ballots was estimated at $40,542 (Congressional Record H6986). It was also estimated/alleged that printing costs doubled in Wyoming, and Nebraska spent over $30,000 in one county to print ballots that no one requested (House Hearing, supra note 61 at 1957–1966, as quoted in Boyd and Markman 1983). It should be noted that many of these concerns were unfounded—data suggest that the costs associated with printing bilingual ballots are grossly overestimated; a 1984 study illustrates that written bilingual material accounted for 7.6 percent of the total election expenditures for all 295 covered jurisdictions (General Accounting Office 1984). The most recent General Accounting Office study of minority language ballots, published in 2008, demonstrates that targeting and other cost-limiting procedures (volunteers, floating bilingual assistants) work to keep expenditures low.

The VRA was amended again in 1982. Prior to this revision, the VRA was perceived to apply only when the laws were enacted or maintained for a discriminatory purpose. It did not cover discriminatory effect. The creation of Section 2 in 1982 protects from discriminatory effects as well as purpose.

Prior to the 2006 reauthorization, *Georgia v. Ashcroft* 2003 addressed racial gerrymandering. As a result, the 2006 reauthorization included a more expansive approach to Section 5, to address racial gerrymandering in states beyond those covered in Section 4(b) of the VRA. *For more details on those expansions, see Reilly (2015).*

The largest challenge to the VRA in recent history was the court case *Shelby County v. Holder* 2013. *Shelby* invalidated Section 5 and Section 4(b) of the VRA that Southern states (with a history of voting discrimination) no longer needed to have their changes to voting laws approved by the federal government. This means that all states have the power to amend their voting laws with no oversight. As a result, seventeen states implemented new voting restrictions for the 2016 election—cutting back early voting, making it increasingly difficult to vote, and requiring strict forms of government-issued identification. These states extended far beyond the South to include some crucial swing states (such as Ohio, Wisconsin, and Virginia)—these states also account for 189 of the electoral votes available in 2016 (Berman 2016). This opened the door for many more electoral changes, regardless of reasoning and method (until challenged in the court system). Moreover, this sets the stage for possible significant repercussions in future elections.

ELECTION RULE CHANGES

What motivates an individual to vote is important for scholars who study democracies to understand. Much of the research on voter turnout has shown that as the cost to vote increases, turnout rates decline (Hershey 2009). One of the most significant barriers that voters may face is whether they will be allowed to vote or be turned away due to their identification. States that require some form of voter identification have proliferated in the past ten (plus) years (Citrin et al. 2014), yet, voter identification laws have been in place since the 1950s. South Carolina became the first state to require that a voter provide some form of identification with a name on it, followed by Hawaii, Texas, Florida, and Alaska (NCSL Voter ID History 2017). Figure 1.1 provides an illustration of the current voter identification laws in the United States.

Whether certain voting mechanisms such as early voting, online registration, same-day registration, and absentee voting increase turnout is a contested issue. While some researchers say that these mechanisms allow a voter greater opportunity to voice their vote (Berinsky 2005; Alvarez, Ansolabehere, and Wilson 2002; Highton 1997, 2004; Knack and White 2004), others argue that they are not mobilizing new voters but rather the continued participation of likely voters (Neely and Richardson 2001; Hancock 2014). As such, if these laws are not encouraging new voters, is the cost and greater stress on election

Voter Identification Laws in Effect in 2019

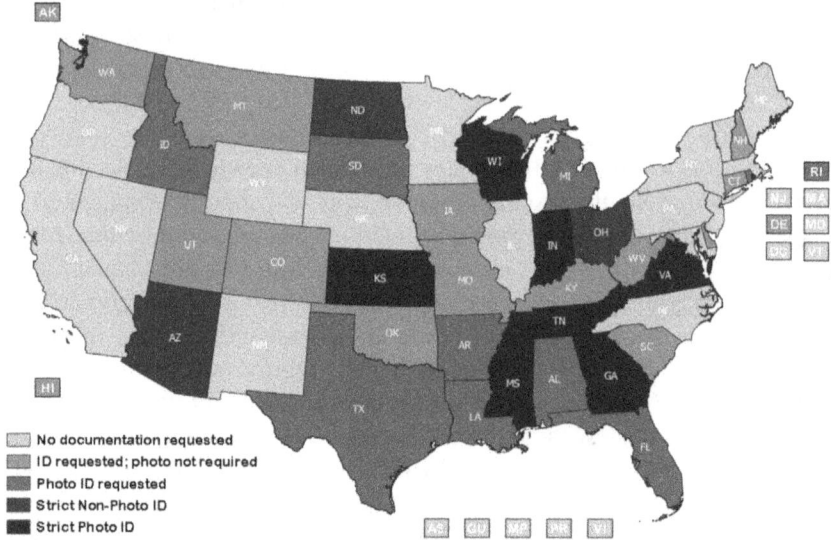

Figure 1.1   **Voting Identification Laws.** Source: Howard 2019.

officials worth it? Whether voter identification requirements do the same is also a contested issue, one that, as we see in the literature, is a discussion that centers on partisan politics (Hicks et al. 2015; McKee 2015; Hicks, McKee, and Smith 2016; Gronke et al. 2015; Biggers and Hanmer 2017). The literature also indicates that there are variations within support for voter identification from legislators beyond partisanship (Hicks, McKee, and Smith 2015; Gronke et al. 2015). Hicks, McKee, and Smith explore the motivations of state legislators from 2005 to 2013 and found that several critical aspects influence support for voter identification laws: high electoral competition, party affiliation, and the racial composition of the lawmaker's district (2015). Gronke et al.'s research focuses on public support finding that voter identification is seen as a way to alleviate voter fraud and protect the integrity of elections (2015). They see variation in support among Democrats based on ideology, education, attention to politics, and racial resentment. Biggers and Hanmer (2017) further suggest that the propensity of adoption of voter identification laws is highest when there has been a shift to Republican control of the governorship and legislature. Yet, a possible explanation of some of these changes to election laws may be merely a function of shrinking state budgets and limited government spending. Now the added challenge of decreasing voter confidence leads to a plausible explanation of the state shifting some expenses and burdens (such as voter identification requirements) to the citizen.

Rocha and Matsubayashi (2013) observed that partisan and racial context is correlated with states adopting strict voter identification requirements. Using duration analysis, they found that Republican governments increase the likelihood of state governments adopting strict voter identification requirements—which was weakened by the size of the minority group. They then used the Current Population Survey (CPS) November Supplemental File for 1980–2010 to observe whether the adoption of such identification requirements affects turnout across racial groups, finding little evidence that minority voter turnout is affected by voter identification requirements. Hicks et al. (2015) sought to evaluate the likelihood that a Republican-controlled state would introduce restrictive voter identification requirements. Using time-series cross-sectional data (state and year as the unit of analysis), they examine voter identification legislation in the United States from 2001 to 2012. The results of this analysis show that not all Republican-controlled governments push for restricting voter identification requirements. Rather, it is a combination of both the partisan control of the legislative (Republicans), and the electoral context that drives a state to enact restrictive voter identification requirements. Though Republicans strongly and positively influence the adoption-restrictive identification requirements, their effect is significantly weaker in electorally noncompetitive states.

Bailey and Katz (2007) also found little evidence of decreased participation by observing aggregate data from the 2000 and 2004 presidential elections, as well as the 2002 and 2006 midterm elections. However, when observing individual-level data from the CPS across the aforementioned elections, they found that strict identification requirements decrease voter participation. In addition, they find that those who experience decreased participation are more likely to be lower-income and less-educated populations, reinforcing the economic consequences to the voter. Vercellotti and Anderson (2006) also observed both aggregate and individual-level data, and find that as voter identification requirements vary, voter turnout also varies. Observation of the aggregate data showed that requirements such as having voters match signatures on file, and the non-photo identification decreases turnout, as compared to states who only require the voter to state their name. In the unfortunate scenario, that a voter is not allowed to cast their vote due to identification restrictions, many states would allow the voter to cast a provisional ballot.

Provisional ballots are a necessary mechanism to ensure that voters are not disenfranchised. They are used when a voter does not appear on the registration rolls (Feige 2005). There are two philosophies regarding provisional ballots: substantive and procedural. The substantive philosophy treats provisional voting the same as same-day registration, in which the voter is provided a provisional ballot (even if they are not registered), which will later be assessed by election officials to ensure that the voter meets all of the necessary requirements to vote. Second, philosophy allows the provisional ballot to be cast only if the voter had already properly registered to vote. The difference between the two lies in the competing notion that even if the voter failed to properly register, they should be afforded the opportunity to cast a ballot (Foley 2004).

Provisional balloting was established through the Help America Vote Act 2002 (HAVA), after voters—who had properly registered—were turned away from the voting booths in 2000, after their names were improperly removed from voter registration lists (Foley 2004). HAVA regulations included improvements in election technology, the implementation of standards that states must meet to protect voter rights, statewide voter registration systems, and voter education programs (Alvarez and Hall 2006; Foley 2004). Following HAVAs enactment, nearly 2 percent of the ballots cast in the 2004 election were provisional. Two-thirds of those provisional ballots were valid and were primarily cast by voters who were not previously registered (Ansolabehere 2007). Yet, not all states count provisional ballots at the same rate (Foley 2008). Although these barriers may have a significant impact on the voter in some states, there are various other ways to circumvent the issue of registration, for instance: same-day and online registration.

Thirteen states plus the District of Columbia offer same-day registration, wherein the voter can show up on Election Day, register, and then vote. To prevent fraud, the voter must provide proof of residency that is often met through the required form of identification, which varies by state (NCSL Same Day Voter Registration 2017). Burden (2014) found a positive relationship between same-day registration and voter turnout. Conducting both individual-level and aggregate statistical analyses of voter turnout in the 2004 and 2008 presidential elections, they found that Election Day registration has a positive and significant effect on increasing turnout.

Online registration is more efficient than paper registration, costs less, and reduces the number of provisional ballots that need to be cast. Thirty-four states, plus the District of Columbia, now allow online registration. Online registration is similar to paper registration, but instead of submitting a paper, the voter submits an electronic form through the internet. Like paper registration, the form is transmitted to election officials, who then validate the information provided with documents such as driver's licenses and other state identifications (NCLS Online Voter registration 2017). Online registration reduces the number of provisional ballots that need to be cast by reducing incomplete registration forms and making the process more efficient. The technology used to process online registration entails protocols that alert the voter if there are incomplete sections, thus reducing Election Day problems. The process is more efficient overall and has the potential to save districts money. Maricopa County in Arizona saved over $1.4 million in 2008, after encouraging its voters to register online. Additionally, online registration has the potential to reach populations that are often underrepresented, for instance, younger voters who are typically internet-savvy users (Cohen 2013). Voter identification and registration barriers are not the only problems that a voter may face on Election Day.

Early voting and absentee ballots are necessary mechanisms to ensure that all voters have a chance to participate in elections. Early voting is defined as "relaxed administrative rules and procedures by which citizens can cast a ballot at a time and place other than the precinct on Election Day" (Gronke, Galanes-Rosenbaum, and Miller 2007: 639). Early voting may entail in-person early voting, vote-by-mail, and no-excuse absentee voting. Early in-person voting is typically held at precincts, although an increasing number of states are now using "satellite locations," which are found at local community centers and local churches. When at the county voting location, the costs can be mitigated as the office is already staffed. However, extended hours and high volume of early voting lead to increased costs for the county due additional staffing requirements. No-excuse absentee voting allows a voter to cast their ballot early, for reasons typically including military duty, students away at college, travel, and hospitalization. Some states (such as California) even offer permanent absentee status. Vote-by-mail allows voters the opportunity to mail in their ballots, a common practice in Oregon, Washington, and Colorado. Voters typically receive their ballots three weeks before the election, and must return them before Election Day. If the voter fails to return the ballot before the Election Day, they have the option to turn it in in-person (Gronke, Galanes-Rosenbaum, and Miller 2007). The literature indicates that this is a cost-saving activity, as voting-by-mail requires fewer Election Day staff. However, the recent changes in state payment of postage for voting-by-mail may increase costs slightly.

While Republicans see voter identification requirements as a necessary mechanism to prevent fraud, Democrats typically view such measures as suppressive. Whether voter identification requirements suppress voter's right is a contested issue as noted earlier. When denied the right to vote at the polls due to registration or identification issues, they may be given the opportunity to cast a provisional ballot—a necessary safeguard. The cost of voter identification is largely borne by the citizen, not the state, as the citizen must get the identification and depending on the type of identification, pay the fee associated with it as well. Online registration, early voting, and absentee voting are just a few of the ways that voters can take action is ensuring that they will be able to cast their vote on Election Day.

In 2005, the Commission on Federal Election Reform recommended that voters provide identification before entering the voting booth. Following the commission's recommendation, states began to enact more strict guidelines for voter identification. Currently, voter identification laws imposed by states can be divided into five categories: (1) No identification required, (2) Non-strict non-photo identification, (3) Non-strict photo identification, (4) Strict non-photo identification, and (5) Strict photo identification (NCSL Voter Identification History 2017). The strict and non-strict aspects of these categories detail what action will be taken if the proper form of identification is not provided. Under *strict guidelines*, a voter without the proper form of identification will cast a provisional ballot and must take additional steps to have their ballot counted (i.e., return with an acceptable ID). *Non-strict* guidelines mandate that the voter will have the option to cast a provisional ballot, without any further requirements. In 2017, seven states require strict photo IDs, three require strict non-photo IDs, ten accept non-strict photo IDs, twelve accept non-strict non-photo IDs, and the remaining use other methods to verify voter identity (NCLS Voter Identification Requirements 2017).

To provide context for this analysis and understanding which laws have been enacted between 2008 and 2017, we have provided table A.1 which depicts the different laws enacted to change voting access in each state as well as the year enacted. The directionality of these laws is important to note—not all changes were a function of restrictions. Some increased accessibility by changing the laws surrounding absentee voting, others on early voting, and online registration. As you will note, many were about the inclusion of voter identification laws that require voters to provide identification to vote and/or register to vote. The 2008–2017 era represents modern voting rights restrictions as a gradual weakening of the VRA has occurred and allowed states greater flexibility in their voting systems even where a history of voting restrictions had previously made alternations difficult or impossible.

OUTLINE OF THE BOOK

Despite the premise and preliminary findings, fiscal restraint was not the only force that limited voting activities post-2008. These findings ultimately made this a tougher book to write but probably better book in the end. By weaving the three-pronged discussion of factors (economic, partisan, and racial) that contribute to the changing electoral laws, we propose the role that threat theory played in this process. The exploration of our theory begins with an examination of several hypotheses that explore our three interconnected explanations of the enactment of these new voting restrictions, while situating them in historical context. We then move into how these connect to threat theory and how it directly applies to modern politics through economics, partisanship, and race to the rise of what we term neo-populists in the Republican

Party and their earlier Tea Party cousins. Using threat theory as the basis, we then turn the mechanism by which concerns over threat become policy instruments, and then turn to the specific policies around voting access. Through each of the chapters, we explore the individual and combined mechanisms to determine their influence on these voting access changes. Finally, an exploration places the restrictions in context in an attempt to understand how they might be elucidated by our three explanatory variables. We then provide a short conclusion to examine the "so what" aspects of these reforms and their effects on participation.

NOTES

1. I should note that I have worked in the area of race and ethnicity before; thus, it was not completely out of my bailiwick but not where I saw this book focusing.

2. Reference to the "one drop rule" is an intended double entendre.

Chapter 2

Threat Theory

Economic, Partisan, and Racial Threats

UNDERSTANDING THREAT AND THREAT RESPONSE

In social and political climates, individuals identify with communities that are often at odds with one another, whether due to perceived or real threats. Integrated threat theory, also called intergroup threat theory, attempts to determine what creates these divides between certain groups—in particular, what leads to prejudice. Much of the literature on social identity theory indicates that association with certain in-groups is highly significant on the individual level, "as dear to us as life itself" due to the security and utility that these labels offer us (Stephan et al. 2009). From an evolutionary perspective, association with a given "coalition" was a matter of personal safety and security, and unfamiliar people outside of an individual's coalition were seen as a threat (Miller 2008). This idea has been broadly applied to populations in an attempt to explain why tensions emerge between certain groups. The next few sections examine the different threat theories and their correspondence within our research.

Categories of Identity Threat

Branscombe et al. (1999) identify four categories of identity threat that lead to friction between groups: "categorization threat" (being unwillingly categorized), "distinctiveness threat" (where distinguishing characteristics of a group's identity are suppressed, rejected, or minimized), "threats to the value of social identity" (a group identity is devalued), and "acceptance threat" (an individual's place in a group is undermined). With this framework in mind, the authors argue, it becomes easier to identify the social situations in which each threat is most likely to occur, as well as how the individuals involved are likely to react. Additionally, Branscombe et al. (1999) argue that different intensity of responses are likely to be expressed by people depending on how strongly they associate themselves with a given group identity.

Categorization Threat

Social categorization has often been described in the literature as a tactic of self-preservation (Miller 2008). In the evolutionary context, this was critical in helping humans avoid dangerous situations, particularly in the form of threatening groups (Öhman and Mineka 2001). Drawing from Cosmides, Tooby, and Kurzban (2003, 2001), Miller (2008) argues that it is likely that developments may have been taken place to allow humans to process cues regarding coalitional associations. This would explain the tendency to categorize into "us" and "them" (Miller 2008). The coalitional mind-set, Miller (2008) writes with support from Cosmides et al. (2003) and Kurzban et al. (2001), identifies race as a strongly divisive factor, one that often shapes "self-protective biases." Moreover, when individuals need to categorize people whose race or politics are not immediately clear, they tend to assign them to the out-group as opposed to their own in-group; threat cues would predictably bias whites to view those of an ambiguous background as being black and not white (Miller 2008).

This categorization leads people to believe that they are being treated and defined unjustly, Branscombe et al. (1999) argue. Categorization, as argued in the psychological literature on this topic, allows for quick processing of identities; qualities are narrowed down, in a sense (Miller 2008). In situations where an individual would expect to be viewed on his independent merits (Branscombe et al. use the example of job interviews), those with a bias against the individual would instead view the individual as a member of his broader category, which often carries many stereotypes and negative associations. That individual is likely to feel that he is the victim of prejudice or discrimination, Branscombe et al. (1999) argue, having been boiled down to perceived gender, ethnicity, or political affiliation.

Distinctiveness Threat

Distinctiveness threat unites the dynamics of self-categorization with the tendency of people to emphasize (perhaps excessively so) the differences between their group and others (Branscombe et al. 1999). Where categorization threat deals with the negative view of categorization and stereotypical or simplified notions of identity, distinctiveness threat describes the friction that can result when social identities are perceived to have been lost, Branscombe et al. (1999) argue. Distinctiveness between social groups leads to survival-based attachment; as groups come into conflict due to their differing interests, members of each will only grow more allegiant to their respective sides, in the view of Tajfel and Turner (1986).

A typical motivating factor for seeking group distinctiveness is the desire to have a structure to guide behavior (Branscombe et al. 1999). Additionally, Branscombe et al. (1999) argue that possessing a distinct identity might matter more to members of an in-group than possessing a positive identity. This is especially true of the members who identify most strongly with a given group. Perceived uniqueness relates directly to how uncommon a group is; that is, numerical distinctiveness (Branscombe et al. 1999). One example is a series of interviews referenced by McGuire, McGuire, and Winton in 1979, which confirmed a hypothesis regarding maleness and femaleness as part of self-concept: boys who came from houses with more females were much more likely to mention maleness as part of their identities (even unprompted), while females exhibited the same tendency in female-dominated households. Individual identities seen as atypical are often the most deeply held, a point that holds steady throughout the literature.

Threats to Value

Branscombe et al. (1999) put forth an interpretation of "threats to value" that has to do with a direct attack from a member of an out-group on the values of the in-group. The out-group isn't always necessarily the direct threat; per Branscombe et al. (1999), it could also be the object of some third party hoping to induce conflict between the in-group and the out-group. In much of the literature, threats to value—which tend to also encompass threats to religion, political ideology, group philosophy, notions of ethics, and so on—tend to be kept separate from more tangible threats (Stephan et al. 2009). Stephan et al. (2009) dub the former as "symbolic group threats" and the latter as "realistic group threats," creating a clear distinction.

The perception of threats to value is seen by many current scholars as being influenced by a group's historical identity. For example, members of an in-group may be reticent to accept an influx of immigrants due to the potential difficulties that may come with assimilation; the very same group of immigrants may fear for the sake of its long-held identity and worry that the host culture would be a threat to their values (Stephan et al. 2009).

The extent to which individuals respond to a threat (real or perceived) depends highly on how associated with a given social group that individual is (Branscombe et al. 1999). Through an analysis of a series of social experiments, Branscombe et al. (1999) put forth a series of claims regarding self-affirmation, confidence in a social group, and reactionary derision of the majority. In one example, Americans were asked to watch a video in which an American boxing opponent lost to a Russian. The strongly identified

Americans privately reported lower feelings of collective pride compared to Americans who were separately assigned to watch a video in which the American beat the Russian (Branscombe et al. 1999). These lower feelings of group pride very directly predicted "out-group derogation," as Branscombe et al. (1999) write—the amount of which predicted increases in self-esteem.

Acceptance Threat

Finally, Branscombe et al. (1999) discuss acceptance threat, a dynamic that the authors view as "pertaining to intragroup processes, albeit in an intergroup context." Acceptance threat derives from an individual feeling that his personal place in his chosen group is being challenged. Two conclusions, per Ross (2016) and his interpretation of social identity theory, follow this definition: individuals tend to align themselves with groups out of personal uncertainty, and after feeling that uncertainty, these individuals are more likely to derogate perceived outsiders (McGregor, Haji, and Kang 2008). This suggests that we create "outgroups" when we feel threatened. McGregor, Haji, and Kang (2008) posit that group biases are powerful because they validate the self-worth and certainty of in-group members, which in turn enables individuals to operate at their social best. It follows that individuals who are more secure in their social identities are less likely to resort to defensiveness or argument when their position within a group is challenged (Sherman and Cohen 2006).

Looking at the opposite dynamic, Branscombe et al. (1999) identify two situations where an individual might resort to those defensive and derogatory tactics: when one tries to join a new group and is shut out, and when one is excluded from a preexisting group. There are any number of tactics that individuals may employ in order to gain acceptance into a desired group. They may have a tendency to differentiate themselves from out-groups in order to appear more attractive to the in-group, acting strategically in their own interests to clearly align themselves with their preferred identity (Branscombe et al. 1999; Turner 1991; Wetherell and Potter 1987). Members of the in-group who feel that their place in that group is insecure or even illegitimate (due to tactics such as exaggeration of qualities in order to gain acceptance) tend to treat out-group members with more hostility than members of the in-group who feel that their place is secure and legitimate (Branscombe et al. 1999; Breakwell 1979).

It follows that there are a variety of psychological processes that shape the behaviors of a group when faced with unfamiliar values, belief sets, and ethics. For example, Croucher (2017) views the refugee crisis in Europe as a prime example of threat theory. As more and more Europeans come to believe that refugees pose an inherent threat to their cultures (whether this is because they come to Europe with their own cultural backgrounds and values perceived to be corrupt, or because they refuse to adopt the native European values), anti-immigrant sentiment and prejudice both rise, and discrimination follows (Croucher 2017). Two broad classes of threats are primarily discussed in current literature: realistic threats and symbolic threats. Realistic threats tend to take on a very tangible form, posing danger to a group's economic or physical safety (Croucher 2017; Stephan et al. 2009). Symbolic threats, on the other hand, threaten the in-group's culture, posing existential dangers as opposed to realistic threats (Croucher 2017; Stephan et al. 2009). In analyses of much of the current political literature regarding threat theory, both symbolic and realistic threats are considered.

Threats can come in various forms. Partisan threat may be determined if the partisan majority is at risk. Economic threat comes when there is an economic downturn that political leaders and citizens see a threat to their well-being. Racial threat comes when there is a perceived threat to one's place in the racial hierarchy. These three threats can be independent or work in conjunction with each other as discussed throughout the rest of the book.

The literature surrounding threat theory identifies different factors as being critical to understanding why prejudices/discomfort emerge. Croucher (2017) summarizes them as follows: "intergroup conflict, status inequalities, strength of in-group identification, knowledge of the out-group, and intergroup contact." The majority of current scholars discuss these qualities, though often labeled differently. Intergroup threat applies these qualities to a broader context, though many of the fears and uncertainties that define intergroup threat theory draw from Croucher's (2017) listed qualities. Branscombe et al. (1999) perform a particularly thorough analysis of the various sources of prejudice between groups, drawing on psychological and sociological principles, as is often the case in the literature on threat theory.

Our review of this literature as detailed earlier dovetails closely with our understanding of the threats that the neo-populists are likely responding to in their policy demands. There are two groups that respond to the threats perceived in societies: political leaders and citizens. Political leaders are likely to enact policy to counter that threat and citizens are expected to vote for those policies (and leaders) that counter the threat. While there are many identifiable impacts of the activation of the threat response, the focus of our examination is on voting access restrictions and why they have become an increasingly common policy tool.

For the public, the activation of the threat response occurs at three levels: the individual, the small group, and the perceived societal level. These levels can be viewed as concentric circles, which radiate outward from the individual and influence their responses. At the most individual level, the impact of the threat activation can be observed in opinion formation where the perceived threat is given form, and is often seen from those groups that are outside of the immediate and personal sphere of the individual. As individuals, leaders, and states evaluate the threat, face the attempt to martial the information they have, and generally turn to their set of experiences, and to a lesser extent, their knowledge as they give form to the threat they face. As they attempt to process the near primal threat response, they behave much like voters are predicted to when facing cognitively intensive problems. Rather than seeking new and better information, most turn to the most readily available information they have: their experiences. As individuals attempt to engage cognitively with this process, they natively turn to the "others"— those that are unlike themselves to give form to the threat.

Here a single negative interaction with the "others" radiates strongly in the low information and cognitively intense processing that a threat represents, and a single negative interaction becomes a heuristic for the larger threat and becomes the basis for how the threat takes form for them. In addition, it is here positive ongoing interactions mitigate the threat response and push threat away from being identified with the positive contact. The perceptions of others can be called upon both among partisans and racial groups—one can even expand that to other social classes. Thus, the threat here can be economic, partisan, and racial.

Why examine these three factors and not others? Certainly partisan and racial factors have already been evaluated to some extent in the literature but not in combination with economics. Internationally, we have seen a great growth in blaming others for economic downturns and the rise of populism as a result. Historically we also have had examples of economic conditions providing for the opportunity to scapegoat and prevention of voting rights. One only needs to look at the German economic devastation after the First World War, which included reparations to Frances and Great Britain under the Treaty of Versailles to see the impact that had on creating racial divides and voter suppression (among other atrocities). For many, however, direct contact with "others" has been neither negative nor positive and so they turn to the next most readily available source for low information processes, namely mediated experiences. When there is no direct individual basis for information processing, the individual turns to mediated presentations from friends and neighbors and those within group, the media, and often, elected officials seen as experts in identifying and dealing with the perceived threats.

Thus, reports of negative interactions with out-groups from those within the same social sphere carry substantial weight as individuals form their response to the perceived threat, and the form that threat takes. Living in the realm of the anecdote as the foundation of information about the source of threat leaves a substantial opening for blame to be placed quickly and squarely on those who are viewed as being different and outside the social sphere of the individual. Often building from these same anecdotes, the politician enters the fray and begins to put policy form to the perceived threat and with direct violence largely (but not entirely) foreclosed in the current era. These anecdotes become the source of action that the threatened individual may use to mitigate the threat and seemingly return to the status quo. It is clear in the wider literature (as well as ongoing reductions in crime rates, economic recession/recovery, increased polarization, and de-facto segregation) that the unlikeliness of substantial negative interactions across groups that these mediated circles become the source of both the definition of the threat and the proposed response to the threat.

Thus far, this theory has been well grounded from the literature in both psychology and political science but has posited few within the ground realities. Further, in what has been covered thus far we have primarily identified in- versus out-group and frequently avoided identifying race and ethnicity as that out-group directly. Our approach here is deliberate, indeed, we believe that the threat theory is at the root of the three possible explanations this book examines economic downturns, partisan concerns, and ultimately race and ethnicity—and that the differing explanations all could seek to mitigate threats given different forms. For economic or cost concerns, the perception is rooted in those who already have access and those without increasing the costs of voting as the peril of other preferred governmental services. As states were faced with decreasing budgets during and after the 2008–2009 recession, they made cuts. Further, many feared the loss of their jobs and did, in fact, lose them as a result of the recession creating tension and looking for someone to blame. For partisan concerns, the threat comes from the rise of the "other" political party, which is likely to serve different constituencies, and be rooted in differing values. The threat of losing seats or even loss of major offices can create tension in voters and state administrators. Finally, the most usual threat connected to threat theory—the role of race and ethnicity—looms in both our own theoretic understanding and in the findings of our empirical analysis.

This book differs somewhat in its origin of the threat perception of other racial and ethnic groups. It is our experience that simple racism while a convenient and, in some ways, a simpler and neater explanation ends up insufficient to explain what would motivate so many governments and individual citizens as they respond to perceived threats. We do not discount the reality of real and substantial racial animus among the American public; we instead believe that animus is better explained through threat theory on various levels than through simple racism. Sadly, this explanation is no better than simple racism in the greater moral universe, as the treatment of the different group remains immoral and often repugnant. However, where pure racism is likely to be sticky and changeable only within generations, we believe that threat activated animus, and may respond in policy instruments more directly.

Thus far, we have considered only the role of the citizen in the threat response approach and have largely viewed the politician and elected official only through that lens, but they represent an essential part of the threat hypothesis we are proposing as they represent the tangible avenue for policy response. For us, the story of the elected official is a common one, where the elected officials either notice or create an opening for policy response by engaging directly with the threat response of the voter. The common refrain about elected officials and politicians is that they act like single-minded seekers of election or reelection and therefore formulate policies that are likely to lead to electoral wins. We take a slightly more nuanced view of the incentives faced by elected officials and using the public choice framework identify that like the voters who elect these politicians have policy preferences and are often interested in doing "good" within the bounds of their electoral interest. So here again, we revert to threat theory and response remains our active motivator.

A darker possibility also emerges as the self-interest of politicians becomes active in the system, that some recognizing the potential ability of the threat response to motivate action. Often action, in the absent of threat, would otherwise not be considered by the individual. Thus, they seek to increase the perceived threat to create a policy opening that would otherwise be nonexistent, and then they can then capitalize on to their own advantage, electoral or otherwise. Those threats can come in many forms and provide cover for other activities both lighter and darker in nature.

It is at the confluence of these realities about politicians and elected officials that we believe lay the origins of restrictions on voting access, a small group of elected officials have found that in identifying or creating at least the perception of threat secures their electoral future, and for some, their ideological preferences for a limited electorate can be achieved. For these groups the threat response of many citizens creates a policy opening for restrictions of voting access, that absent the perception of threats to the status quo would be unlikely to garner significant support among the wider population.

As we noted we began this book with a set of expectations about what we would find, our interest was sparked by a puzzle we observed. Why in the decade since 2008 have voting rights restrictions become one of the core issues in nearly every election? The 2008 election was a potentially momentous electoral contest that ended with the first African American president elected in the United States. As a result of this election, the expectations of our electoral system are high and these limitations, targeted as they are, challenge these expectations and results.

The expansion of the franchise and the expansion of access to the voting box had for decades enjoyed widespread and deep support among a citizenry that viewed the political rights attendant to voting as being central to the civic life and culture of the United States. It had seemed that the voting mechanism and directly accessing the ballot box was among those sacrosanct features of civic democracy, hard fought for many disenfranchised groups in the latter half of the twentieth century. Even as this hard fought right was being canonized, cracks were emerging in the perception and view of the importance of elections that would lay the foundation for a new round of voting access restrictions and limitations.

Even a short perusal of the post-Civil War period, with its now-familiar Jim Crow restrictions on voting access that persisted well into the twentieth century, shares a similar message. This message is one of risk and security, particularly the risk of allowing unprepared and unengaged newly minted citizens to participate in the electoral process, and has policy—economic and partisan—consequences. The historical record is replete with the contemporary accounts of the passage of voting access restrictions based on these claimed concerns of the potential risk of allowing open access to the ballot box, and claims of dire outcomes for the culture, and status quo if a liberal view of voting access was applied.

With this theory of threat and using certain threats as cover for other motivations, we developed several hypotheses that address these threats both individually and collectively.

HYPOTHESES

The cost of elections to the state had skyrocketed. The 2016 presidential election cost state and local governments $6.5 billion and the midterm elections in 2018 cost $5.7 billion (NCSL 2018a). Aggregated state budgets in 2018 were $1.94 trillion meaning that the election costs represent around 0.3 percent of the state budgets (NCSL 2018b). While not insignificant, the rising costs of elections—everything from voting equipment, printing of ballots, voter information, and election administration—continue to affect shrinking state budgets. Several states have mandated studies into the cost of elections (Washington, Colorado, California, North Dakota, and Wisconsin) and others passed legislation in 2018 to mitigate the costs of elections (Arizona, Hawaii, Indiana, California, and Michigan) (NSCL 2018b).

There are also different types of electoral laws that we examine in this analysis. Looking at voter identification, the fiscal aspect is neutral as there is limited additional cost to the state, as the cost of providing identification falls onto the voters themselves. We include this in our analysis to demonstrate the differences in how these tools are used vis-à-vis economic, partisan, and racial components. If there were not an economic connection, we would expect that our hypothesis would be null when discussing these types of voter laws. Online registration decreases the cost to the state (after the initial startup costs) as there is less paper to be printed and processed. Finally, early voting or absentee ballots should result in a modest increase to the state, as it requires additional employee hours to staff and process these activities. Given the situational development discussed, it is critical to look at budgets and revenue to understand the implications of voting costs.

Hypothesis 1 proposes a relationship between state budget contractions and spending on election activities. As state budgets contract, one would expect to see a contraction in spending on election activities—particularly voter conveniences such as early voting and absentee ballots as they are seen as more expense to the state and local governments (see earlier discussion of legislative proceedings). Conversely, we should see increases in online registration activities as this leads to decreased costs for state and local governments—particularly with the expectation of HAVA on state governments to maintain the voters' list.

Hypothesis 1: If there is a decrease in state budgets, there will be a decrease in spending on election activities.

We explore changes in state revenues have on voting restrictions in Hypothesis 2. We should also expect to see variations in which types of voting restrictions are adopted and which consolidations or cost-saving methods are utilized. Both budgets and revenues play a role in which of these programs are implemented. However, in Hypothesis 1 we explore state budgetary changes. Budgets were not the only fiscal activity impacted by the 2008–2009 recession, rather, revenue also changed. Since decreasing state revenues, from taxes and other revenue sources, also influenced state's fiscal health as such, it is expected that there will be a decrease in services because of that decreased revenue.

Hypothesis 2: If there is a decrease in state revenue, there will be an increase in voting restrictions.

Finally, we talk about fiscal responsibility in policy innovation (namely online voter registration) and how in times of economic contraction states will turn to cost-efficient voting activities to reduce state costs associated with voting in Hypothesis 3.

Hypothesis 3: If there is a decrease in state revenue, there will be an increase in cost-efficient voting activities (online registration).

Hypothesis 3b: If there is a decrease in state revenue, there will be a decrease in the most costly voting activities (Absentee and Early Voting).

Current conditions tell us that Republican leadership (as well as executive offices) currently dominates many of the state legislatures. As such, to maintain their powerbase (much like partisan power before), we expect that there will continue to be changes to voter access to advantage the governing party. Thus, voting restrictions will be enacted to maintain the powerbase of this party despite the higher number of registered Democrats in the United States. Frankly, one of the only ways to maintain this powerbase is to suppress Democratic voters. Thus, we propose Hypothesis 4 to test party control of the legislature and passage of voting restrictions.

Hypothesis 4: If there is Republican control of the legislature, then there will be an increased voting restrictions.

Similarly, because of the role the executive branch plays in determining electoral policy—either through legislative efforts, executive action, or even through their election officers—we expect that the party in control of the executive branch will have a role in the enactment of the voting restrictions. Secretary of states' offices are often both elected and part of the executive branch at the state level. These partisan offices have direct influence over the electoral laws in the state and administer the rules and regulations around election. As such, it is critical to examine both aspects of the executive branch in this analysis. As a result of this argument, we propose Hypothesis 5 to test this relationship.

Hypothesis 5: If there is Republican control of the executive branch, then there will be an increase in voting restrictions.

While partisan control of one branch may influence the successful passage of legislation, total partisan control of both the legislature and the gubernatorial office may be additionally successful. This, in combination with partisan control of the CEO, may actually result in substantive changes in voting policies. Thus, if we look at Republican control more specifically (consistent with the literature and Hypotheses 4 and 5), we should expect that when Republicans hold all offices in the state that have electoral relevance, there will be an increase in voting restrictions. This relationship of total partisan control is proposed in Hypothesis 6.

*Hypothesis 6: If there is Republican control of multiple branches of govern-
ment, then there will be an increase in voting restrictions.*

Finally, we also expect that the percent of vote in the previous election will
influence the enactment of these laws. Those who received a higher margin of
victory will be less likely to enact voter restrictions, as their reelection is more
likely than those with a low margin of victory. Those with a low margin may
want to discourage voters of the other party form participating. The role of
party competition and the margin of victory is well examined in the literature
(e.g., Abramowitz 1991; Jacobson 1989; Lublin 1994). We seek to add how
this contributes to voting restrictions. Suggesting that when legislators feel
additional pressure/threat to their reelection with low margins of victories
they will also want to ensure their place in the legislature by preventing members of the opposition party from voting. This leads us to Hypothesis 7 to test
the impact of margin of victory on future voting restrictions.

The 2016 election and the 2018 elections demonstrate the value of the margin of victory. The 2016 presidential race saw several close states (Florida,
Ohio, Michigan, Wisconsin, and Pennsylvania) separated by less than 2
percent of the vote. Of course, the popular vote nationwide was also close
with 2 percent separating the two major party candidates. At the state level,
this is measured by the top statewide race on the ballot—in 2018, there were
several very close races that made headlines: gubernatorial races in Ohio
and Texas were separated by less than 5 percent of the vote; Florida's and
Georgia's gubernatorial races were separated by less than 2 percent margin.
There were additional races at the state level that were separated by less than
fifty votes in Illinois, Florida, Minnesota, Iowa, Washington, and Idaho. The
Alaska House race between Bart LeBon and Kathryn Dodge was separated
by one vote. The closeness of these elections demonstrates that there may be
a desire to increase the margin by voter suppression of the other party leading
us to Hypothesis 7.

*Hypothesis 7: If there is a low margin of victory, then there will be an
increase in voting restrictions.*

The examination of racial discrimination in voting laws leads us to the
examination of three interrelated hypotheses. First, in Hypothesis 8 we look
broadly at the role that minority populations play in determining voting
restrictions. We then examine two related hypotheses—first looking at black
populations where we know there is a historical development of laws that
have purposefully targeted this population in Hypothesis 8a. We also examine the changes vis-à-vis the Latino population given the increased rhetoric
around immigration and Latino voters in Hypothesis 8b. There is a growing

literature on the disenfranchisement of Latino voters through voter identification laws (e.g., Hajnal, Lajevardi, and Nielson 2017; Wang 2012; Barreto, Nuno, and Sanchez 2007) that contributes to this argument.

Hypothesis 8: If there is a high percentage of minority population in a state, then there will be more voting restrictions.
Hypothesis 8a: If there is a high percentage of the black population in a state, then there will be more voting restrictions.
Hypothesis 8b: If there is a high percentage of Latino population in a state, then there will be more voting restrictions.

THE INTERSECTION

Our theoretical expectations show the intertwining of three factors that contribute to the change in voting laws that have occurred since 2008. The literature clearly supports racial and partisan motivation but ignores the economic impact of the recession on these voting restrictions. While we suggest there is independent relationship, there is also an interactive effect from these three factors. Therefore, we propose this intertwined theory that examines economic factors, partisanship, and racial threat as contributors to the changes we see. As our introduction demonstrates, our focus was initially simply economics but that was misguided and a little shortsighted. Economics certainly plays a role in the decisions around spending but also as cover for nefarious motives.

While we hypothesized the effects individually earlier, there is clear intersectionality between these three causes. Policy is not created in a vacuum—thus, there is often an interaction of these factors that contribute to the decision and policy-making processes. Clearly, fiscal restraint, partisanship, and racism may be considered strange bedfellows; however, their connection is undeniable.

We consider how threat activation leads to the development of voting restrictions' policies. Our belief is that the policy opportunity comes from the interaction between the threat responses of the citizenry and how elected officials respond to their perception of the supposed threat. In the following sections, we build from different theories of threat to illustrate the role that all three of these factors have in contributing to why different groups feel threatened enough to enact voting restrictions.

This multiplicity of explanations has been explored in our threat theory discussion and appears to be active in the formation of policy preferences for the majority of the Republican coalition. It is the desire for partisan victory that has allowed the different parts of the coalition to act in concert to influence policy formulation and the actions of Republican elected officials. In examining this potential motivation, we have explored the process by which the wide variation in motivations has been reconciled and these groups have come to be part of the Republican coalition. Our understanding of this process is rooted in the same motivations and approaches first illustrated by the economist Bruce Yandle in his exploration of odd bedfellows that have come to be called Baptists and Bootlegger coalitions, and the extensions of that work that detail how political entrepreneurs actively work to create the coalitions necessary to advance policy positions (Yandle 1983). In this case, we propose that fiscally conservative motivations may act as the Baptists providing socially acceptable cover for the policy goals of other members of the coalition, especially the Alt Right and other racially focused or nativist elements in the wider party's coalition.

We set out in the next three chapters to explore these factors both individually and in concert. As you will note, we provide several quotes from politicians to demonstrate the use of economics to justify many of their actions, which could cover a number of alternative motivations.

Chapter 3

Voting Restrictions and the Recession

As discussed earlier, the cost of elections is a continuing moving target—not only with different electoral activities but also with the cost to state and local governments to keep up with changing technology and upgrading voting machinery. Thus, what role did the 2008–2009 recession have on trying to mitigate these costs? Could it be that election administrators were focused on the cost of election activities and attempted to mitigate the looming threat to their state and local budgets by restricting election services (e.g., early voting) or passing the cost onto voters (e.g., voter identification)?

The recession in 2008–2009 provided the catalyst for many state budget contractions. These contractions were felt across policy areas—including election funding. While these contractions were not felt equally across states, they were indeed felt with different government spending cuts. I suggest that fiscal contraction and the recession led specifically to these cuts. Alternatively, we would expect that when there are contractions in the government spending, cost efficiencies would be explored. As a result, we would expect that state governments would embrace online voter registration to mitigate costs, if there is a truly fiscal or economic purpose behind these laws.

UNDERSTANDING FISCAL CONSERVATISM

Fiscal conservatism and its resulting policy impact have a long history in American politics and the policy discussions, and voting rights and the administration of elections are not exceptions. Fiscal conservatism is characterized by concerns over spending, taxation, and in general the resources that are used by government programs. These concerns have long been core to most policy discussions in US history and evidence can be found in nearly every policy discussion. The roots of what has become modern fiscal conservatism can be found throughout most American policy decisions from the beginning of the republic. As early as the discussion over the Articles of Confederation, fiscal conservatism and its attendant focus on spending and revenue have dominated policy conflicts. These concerns over spending levels (including: maintaining low taxes, searching for balanced budgets, and attempts to reign in the growth of government programs) while not always the dominant argument in policy decisions, can almost always be identified in the policy discussion. This reality has been solidified in discussions covering a wide range of policy issues from welfare to defense and likely extending to the policy discussions surrounding election administration and voting access.

One of the clearest examples of the influence of fiscal conservatism's role in the Republican Party can be seen in the "Contract with America" that dominated politics in the mid-1990s. The contract essentially pledged congressional Republicans to spending, taxes, and ultimately a balanced budget. These pledges were the primary concerns that the party and influenced many policy choices. This era of the mid-1990s, likely represents the height of the dominance of the Fiscal Conservatives in the Republican coalition. Since the 1990s, other parts of the coalition have risen (and fallen) in prominence. In the post-9/11 era, war hawks and security-focused conservatism seemed to dominate the agenda of the party, and foreign policy and terrorism were primary issues. Despite this change in dominating focus, the questions of the Fiscal Conservatives were not far behind. And while not the primary motivator, in the policy discussion, questions over fiscal policy and circumstance were raised repeatedly during the both the immediate Iraq war and the larger war on terror that resulted (Huber and Espenshade 1997).

While it would clearly be overstating to suggest that fiscal concerns won the policy day during this era, the concerns of Fiscal Conservatives were readily identifiable in the policy discussions. Similarly even at the height of the mid-2000s financial crisis, discussions of fiscal issues including spending and taxes were part of what fueled the rise of the Tea Party. This led to the defeat of numerous Republican incumbents who were viewed as having violated at least in part (according to the Tea Party) the norms of fiscal conservatism that had dominated. The costs of Emergency Economic Stabilization Act in particular were among the most discussed parts of the policy response in the post-2009 era.

As is illustrated by the two examples earlier, it is clear that even among the most controversial policy discussions of the recent past fiscal conservatism has remained a substantial and influential influence on the policy process, although the faction has not always dominated in final policy decisions. Given the consistent influence of the fiscal conservatism across policy domains in the Republican Party, we would expect that election administration and voting rights access would similarly be impacted by discussions of fiscal issues.

FISCAL STRESS, FISCAL CONSERVATISM, AND POLICY RESPONSE

Among the most interesting moments to observe fiscal conservatism in action is during times of fiscal stress as policy makers and elected officials attempted to combat economic issues with policy responses. In general, the responses of Fiscal Conservatives to economic recessions have been reduction in tax burdens in an attempt to spur economic growth. This means tax incentives to corporations to create more jobs and give Americans additional financial security. The 2008–2009 economic recession, however, illustrated that the Republican coalition responded to the downturn by turning to policy responses that attempted to blame "others" for the economic stress. This provided an opportunity not only to address economic threats but to assert who was to blame for the economic threats. Additional threats are envisioned in jobs moving overseas, immigrants (skilled and unskilled) perceived as taking jobs from Americans and even blaming "out groups" for the economic situation (rather than subprime mortgage rates and other government fiscal policies) for the economic recession. Thus, as the nativist and Alt Right portions of the Republican coalition were activating through threat theory, Fiscal Conservatives were likewise activated. Absent the fiscal stress (like the recession), Fiscal Conservatives are unlikely to view immigrants or other minorities as a threat. When the potential costs of policies are generally supported by these groups, these issues become salient and these threats are thrust in the policy discussion. These concerns become cover for the policy preferences of the less seemly parts of the coalition.

In particular, we would expect that during times of increased fiscal stress those fiscal concerns would be more prevalent in the discussion and that coupled with racial and partisan influences more likely to occur. However, we would expect that the support of Fiscal Conservatives would be limited to those actions that reduce or prevent increased spending. Thus, we expect that differing electoral administration policy changes would be more likely to occur as result.

EXAMPLES OF FISCAL IMPACTS ON ELECTION
ADMINISTRATION AND VOTER ACCESS

While there is substantial real-world evidence of both partisan and racial impact on election administration and policy decisions about voter access across the popular and academic literature, there is a dearth of examinations of the potential impact of fiscal considerations (included in brief earlier). Despite this dearth of literature, there is some evidence that elected officials are weighing the fiscal concerns and particularly the costs of voter access when making these policy decisions.

One such example comes from a 2014 attempt to increase early voting in Missouri. Amendment 6 which the Missouri Legislature placed on the ballot would have created greater access to voting precincts and could vote by mail for six business days prior to an election, ending on the Wednesday immediately prior to the election. The attempt was expected to cost the state and local jurisdictions at least $2 million (Hancock 2014). David Kimball, a political science expert in the area of election administration, was quoted as saying that he did not see the Republican legislature in Missouri as willing to sign off on that type of expenditure. Further, he wondered about the true impact of allowing additional early voting on participation rates, as many early voters were doing so out of convenience but would likely vote anyway (Hancock 2014). Similarly, Kay Brown (Christian County clerk and then president of the Missouri Association of County Clerks) and other election authorities raised significant concerns about this cost while expressing support for the general notion of increasing voter access. When asked about it, Brown responded, "someone has to pay for it, and it would have a dramatic impact on the cost of running an election" (Hancock 2014). Republican Missouri state representative Tony Dugger reiterated this concern over increased costs saying, "when you throw early voting into the mix, you're increasing the cost of elections and the workload on local offices" (Hancock 2014). Dugger also hoped that if early voting passed, the state legislature funds it fully rather than passing those costs on to the counties.

A similar attempt to increase early voting in New Jersey in 2013 drew similar concerns. Governor Christie commenting in his veto message on the bill, said that while vote by mail had proven effective and cost effective, early voting would have cost New Jersey taxpayers about $25 million dollars each year (Sieger 2014). Likewise, local elected officials expressed concerns about early voting becoming an unfunded mandate imposed on local governments. One local elections official commenting on the potential for the state to cover the costs of early voting stated, "if the state doesn't have the money for the services the state has traditionally provided like human services, why do we need to dream up other ways to spend this money" (Sieger 2014).

This illustrates not only concern about costs but also who would bear the cost of these changes. The cost of early voting is also difficult to calculate when there are fiscal returns that influence Election Day. While the expectation is a dramatic increase in costs borne by early voting, some of this is mitigated by utilizing offices already open on Election Day, and that those who cast early ballots limit the burden on Election Day by requiring fewer officials and less equipment. In Johnson County, Kansas, more than half of all voters cast early ballots in 2008 (through extended office hours and weekend voting) which enabled the county to reduce the number of polling locations on Election Day (Hancock 2014). Thus, the fiscal impacts of election changes are not unidirectional and each type of election change needs to be examined separately in our analysis. While these are anecdotal stories surrounding expanded election, access can serve only as illustrations of the way local officials think about increased voting access, a more detailed study by the National Conference of State Legislatures explored the cost sensitivity and awareness of state legislatures to the cost. They concluded that the costs of electoral reform were salient to the decision-making of elected officials when considering making electoral reforms (NCSL 2018b).

As noted earlier, the exact cost of election administration and the additional cost created by any single policy are notoriously difficult to measure. Several levels of government have a role in running and paying for elections (including state, counties, municipalities and even special districts) (NCSL 2018b). With the role that counties, cities, and townships play in the election process, it means that there could be more than 10,000 jurisdictions running election in the United States (not including subdivisions) (NCSL 2018b). The state has had a consistent and lengthy role in the election process, particularly after the passage of Help America Vote Act (HAVA). HAVA requires a computerized statewide voter registration list to be maintained at the state level. States have discretion as to the mechanisms they use to maintain this list but the cost of the system is a responsibility of the state with some funding assistance from HAVA appropriations. Table A.2 provides a listing of what states pay for in different types of elections.

The NCSL's study of the costs of elections attempted to bring together the varied approaches that the states used to finance the costs of elections and the manner in which they were paid. In most cases, the state acts as the financial guarantor and overseer of the electoral process while local government entities, most often counties, act as the organizer and facilitator of the actual process of voting. Given this institutional arrangement, we would expect that state legislators, in the role of appropriator, might be particularly sensitive to voting access changes that would increase costs and lead to local governments clamoring for increased electoral funding.

While we would expect them to be sensitive to those costs, we would expect that given the relatively small costs of election when compared to other budgetary items, their concerns would become a relevant part of the decision process primarily when fiscal conditions are poor and budgetary conditions are tight. It is under these circumstances that Fiscal Conservatives (from both parties) are likely to be willing to prioritize control of electoral administrative costs, thus making Fiscal Conservatives more willing to respond to calls from others in the coalition to limit voting access.

The Great Recession started in December 2007 and lasted until June 2009. This had more effect on state budgets than any previous economic downturn (Gordon 2012). While there was a rebounding effect after 2009, it lagged two to three years. Moreover, this impacted property taxes and resulted in cutbacks to local government transfers. However, the American Recovery and Reinvestment Act of 2009 also provided "unprecedented fiscal relief to states and localities limiting the pressure on state governments" in the long term (Gordon 2012).[1] There was, however, a sharp decline in state revenues (across sales, income and property taxes) (US Census Bureau, Quarterly Tax Survey 2011). There was also a resulting increase in demand for state services—Unemployment Insurance and Medicaid (US Department of Labor, Employment and Training Administration: Health Insurance Coverage in the United States). While some states increased taxes to pay for the shortfall, many reduced their spending. Cuts fell predominantly in education, health, and social services (Gordon 2012). These cuts continue, albeit some have been alleviated by tax collection. States have been reluctant to increase or even maintain ongoing spending. The Government Accountability office (2012) has projected that by 2060 there will be a 2–4 percent of GDP gap between revenues and spending. There is also an expected public pension funding shortfall of more than $3 trillion at the state and local levels (Oliff, Mai, and Palacios 2012).

STATE BUDGETS

Certainly, state budgets have various influences, and state revenues, resources, and expenditures differ in each of the fifty states. The political environment also contributes to fiscal policy choices at the state level (Poterba 1994; Henisz 2004; Groseclose and McCarty 2001; Baqir 2002).

Poterba's research is of particular interest as he includes variables such as fiscal shock and state political factors over time. He suggests that factors such as divided party control and tax and expenditure limitations affect a state's ability to respond to fiscal shock (1994). This is echoed by Urban Institute. They examine revenue and expenditure changes under fiscal shock and the role of party control, balanced budget requirements, and tax and expenditure limitations (Rueben, Randall, and Boddupalli 2018). Fiscal institutions are also reliant on their interactions with political activities and even the proximity to the election cycle. Issues of veto, tax and expenditures limits, supermajority budget requirements, and divided government all influence state tax and spending policies (Besley and Case 2003). Thus, the budget process is highly political and leads to partisan influences on budget priorities. As such, how much the state spends on election activities is not an arbitrary process—there are a number of budgetary and partisan constraints that lead to the current levels of spending on election processes, as well as a number of requirements of election activities (and consequentially spending).

In this chapter, we explore these three hypotheses to examine the role the economic threat played in the decrease in voting access. These provide the opportunity to explore the role that economic factors played in driving the decisions to change voting laws. Null results should demonstrate (to some extent) that arguments about economic reasons for limited voting activities are providing support for the idea of cover for other causal variables. With this in mind, we examine these three hypotheses.

Hypothesis 1: If there is a decrease in state budgets, there will be a decrease in spending on election activities.

Hypothesis 2: If there is a decrease in state revenue, there will be an increase in voting restrictions.

Hypothesis 3: If there is a decrease in state revenue, there will be an increase in cost-efficient voting activities (online registration).

METHODS

To conduct our analysis (in this and subsequent chapters) we collected date from fifty states for an eighteen-year period between 2000 and 2017. We chose this period to provide time before and after the recession but also to encapsulate changes from HAVA (2002) and *Shelby* (2013). All of these events are significant to our analysis of voting restrictions. As such, the period seemed obvious.

We have five variables representing election-related laws, coded in part based on the definitions provided by the National Conference of State Legislatures. Three of these are ordinal variables. Voter identification is the first law-type of this analysis, coded as an ordinal variable, as follows: 1 = No ID required to vote; 2 = Non-Strict, non-photo ID required to vote; 3 = Non-strict photo ID required to vote; 4 = Strict non-photo ID required to vote; and 5 = Strict photo ID required to vote (this coding is consistent with the NSCL). The distinction between a strict and non-strict ID requirement is based on whether a voter without appropriate identification is prevented from casting a valid ballot (either directly or through casting a provisional ballot which would require later verification of identity) or is allowed to cast a valid ballot (typically signing a document testifying their identity). Early voting is the second voting law analyzed in this study, which captured how long before an election a voter could cast a ballot. This variable is coded based on duration as follows: 0 = no early voting, 1 = early voting starting one to fifteen days before the election, 2 = early voting starting sixteen to thirty days before an election, and finally 3 = early voting starting greater than thirty days before the election. Thus, as this increases the law makes voting more accessible to voters. Permanent absentee status is also included, showing whether or not a state maintained a list of voters who would automatically receive absentee ballots for each election they could vote in. This variable is coded: 0 = no permanent absentee list, 1 = restricted absentee list, and 2 = unrestricted absentee list. The distinction between a restricted and unrestricted absentee list is based on the scope of valid applicants. Some states only allow certain individuals (e.g., wounded veterans or the chronically ill) to apply for such lists, while others allow any voter to do so without qualifications.

The other two election laws used as dependent variables are online registration and no-excuse absentee voting. The former looks at whether online registration exists in the state. The latter policy is defined by whether voters needed an approved purpose to cast an absentee ballot. Both are coded dichotomously with 0 = no enactment and 1 = enactment.

All but one of these election law dependent variables are coded based on year of enactment—a decision which reflects a focus on discovering the sources and timing of restrictive voting conditions. Online registration is the exception to this. In some states, the systems of registration are under the full authority of the secretary of state or equivalent chief election official. Online registration is at times implemented before or entirely without accompanying legislation. For a few cases when online registration is implemented without legislative enactment, the date of implementation is used for coding purposes.

The next set of data utilized in our analysis are the explanatory independent variables. In order of presentation in the text, the economic variables constitute the first set. Specifically, the percentage change in state revenues and state expenditures are included to test the effects of budget pressures on the voting legislation. The economic variables are collected from the Annual Survey of State Government Finances (US Census 2018a). They make a distinction between "general" revenues/expenditures and "total" revenues/expenditures. The "total" qualifier is self-evident, but the "general" statistic concerned only those finances which state institutions had discretion over. Among these, the latter is chosen for inclusion in the analyses, as nondiscretionary funds are by nature difficult to budget and are unlikely to affect other budgetary concerns.

Using the 2008–2013 data, we conducted an analysis to show the short-term impacts of the recession on voting barriers. *Shelby County v. Holder* occurred in 2013 and changed the landscape of many voting rights issues. Thus, a short-term analysis of these issues illustrates the power of the recession in figure 3.1. The following figures examine cross-tabulations in figure form to demonstrate the relationship between the variables.

In figures 3.1–3.4, I examine the relationship between key economic variables and voter identification laws. In figure 3.1, the effect of expenditure

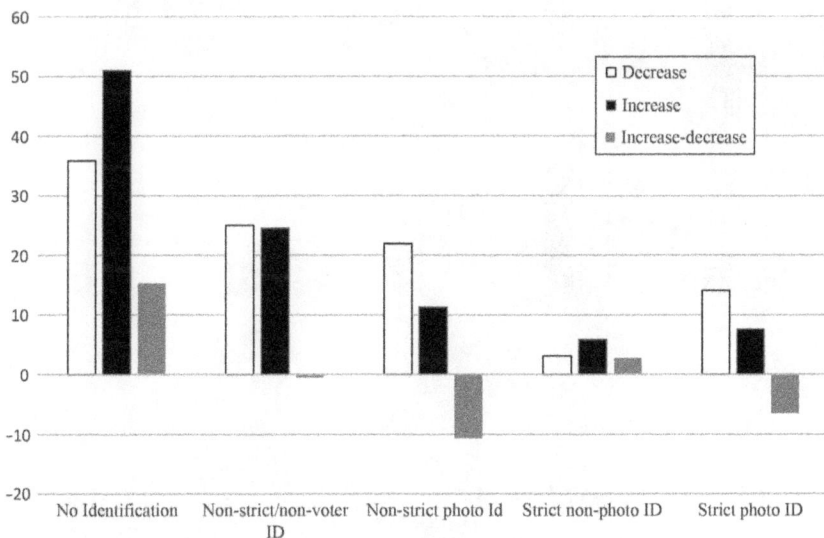

Figure 3.1 **Expenditure Change and Voting Laws.** Author.

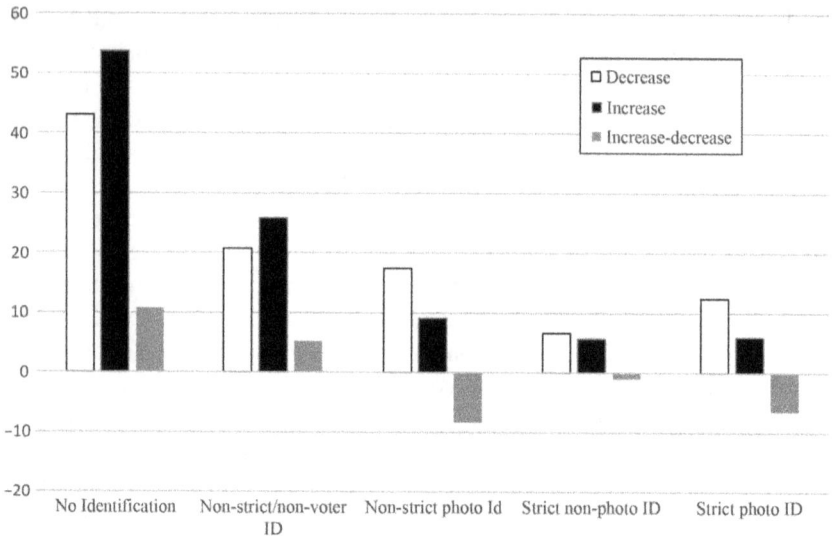

Figure 3.2   Revenue Change and Voting Laws. Author.

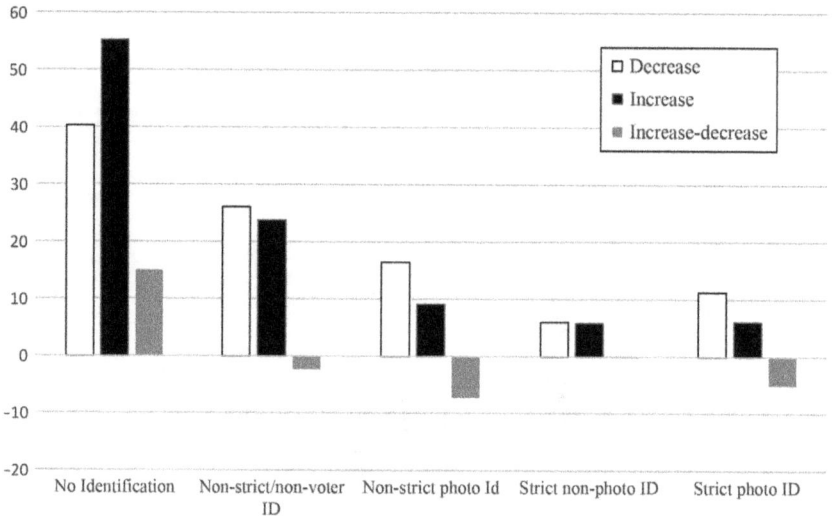

Figure 3.3   GDP and Voting Laws. Author.

change is evaluated. From this analysis, photo identification is required when there is a decrease in expenditures by the states—providing support for Hypothesis 1 as there is a strong connection between the use of photo identification and a decrease in expenditures. Voters are baring the cost of identification to increase electoral security when there is a decrease in government expenditures. Furthermore, that relationship is consistent when

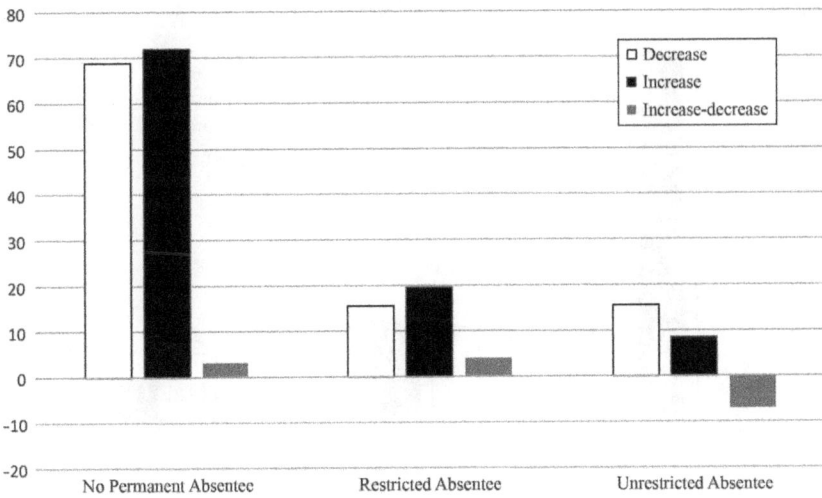

Figure 3.4 Expenditure and Absentee Voting. Author.

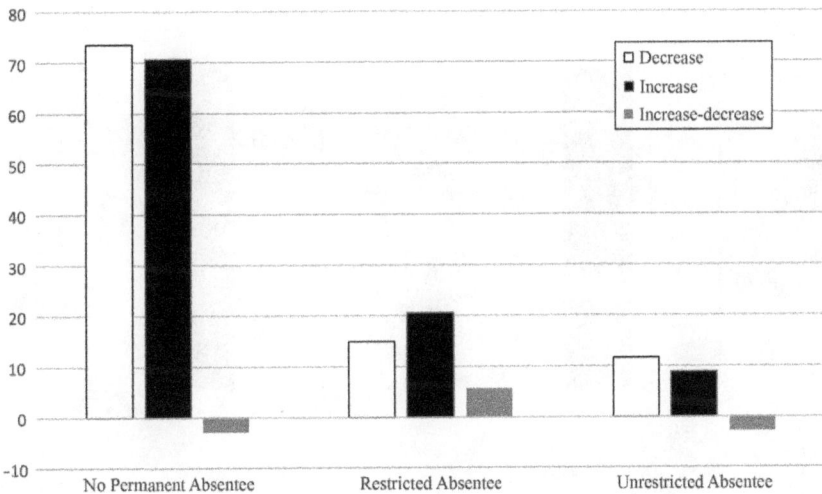

Figure 3.5 Revenue and Absentee Voting. Author.

looking at revenue change and changes in GDP spending in figures 3.2 and 3.3, respectively (supporting Hypothesis 2).

In figure 3.4, we see there is a change in the relationship between spending and absentee ballots. When looking at absentee voting it appears that both decreases in expenditures (figure 3.4), revenue (figure 3.5), and GDP spending (figure 3.6) lead to increases in absentee voting. Demonstrating that when there is actually a decrease in state expenditures, revenues, and GDP

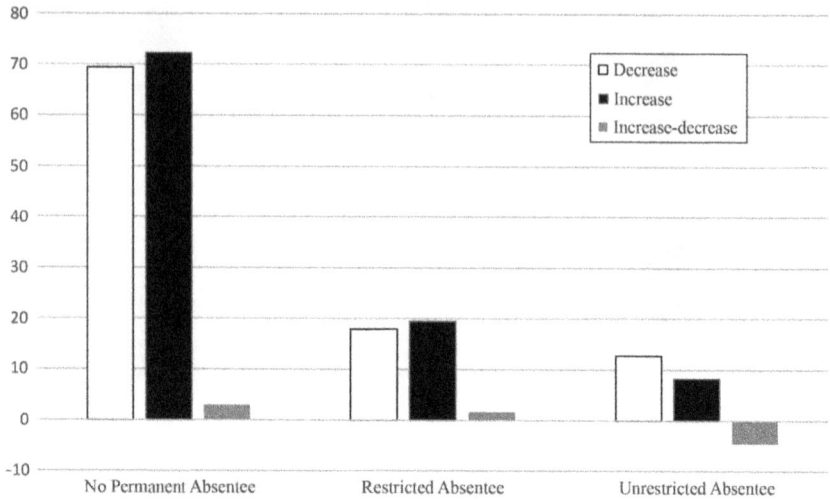

Figure 3.6   GDP and Absentee Voting. Author.

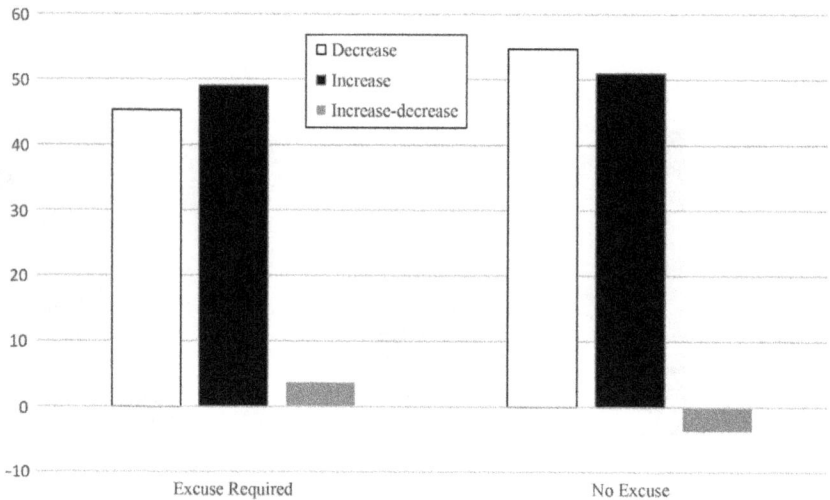

Figure 3.7   Expenditures and No-Excuse Absentee. Author.

there is more likely to be unrestricted absentee (which does increase costs to the states). This is further examined in no-excuse absentee laws. In figures 3.7–3.9, there is increased variation on this relationship. In regard to expenditures, in figure 3.7, as there is a decrease in expenditures, there is an increase in use of no-excuse absentee. Now, no-excuse means fewer administrative hurdles so that fits with the decrease in funding resulting in less bureaucratic work. This relationship holds when looking at GDP (in figure 3.9). However,

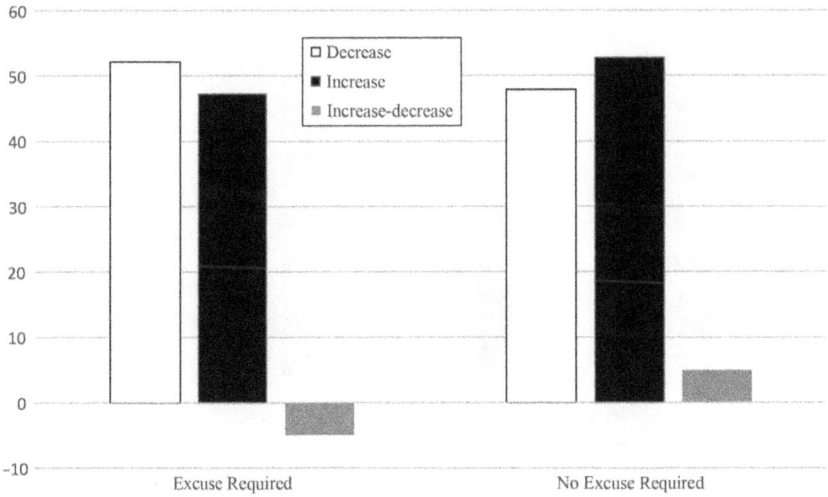

Figure 3.8   Revenues and No-Excuse Absentee. Author.

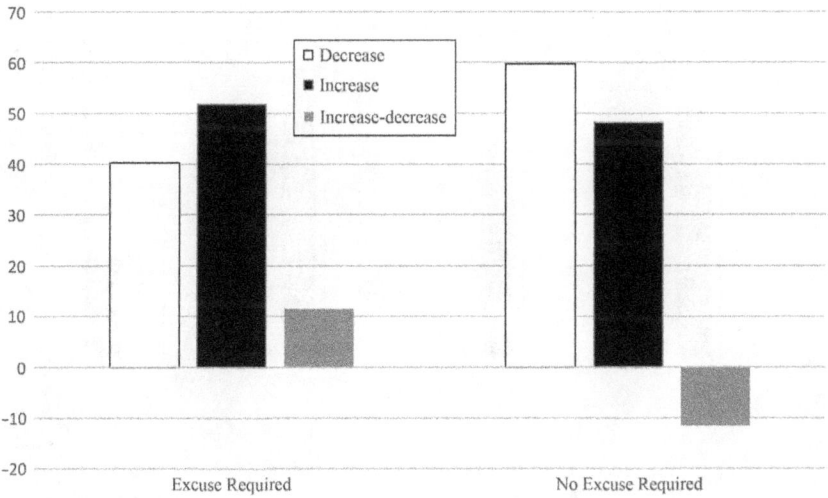

Figure 3.9   GDP and No-Excuse Absentee. Author.

the reverse of this relationship is true when it comes to revenues (in figure 3.9). Thus, the fiscal impact is mixed when looking at absentee voting and needs further analysis.

Looking at one of the more expensive voting laws—early voting—we see that relationship is inconsistent when there is an decrease in expenses (figure 3.10), revenue (figure 3.11), and GDP spending (3.12). For figure 3.10, early voting is restricted in two of the categories (early voting one to fifteen days

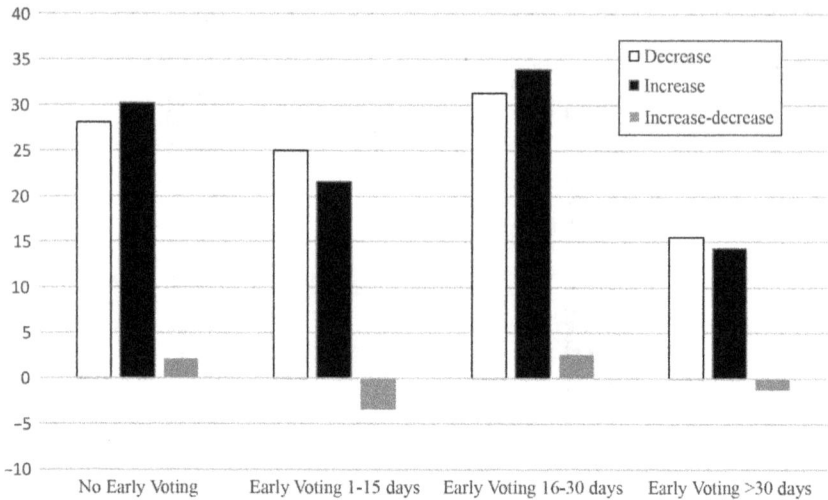

Figure 3.10   Expenditures and Early Voting. Author.

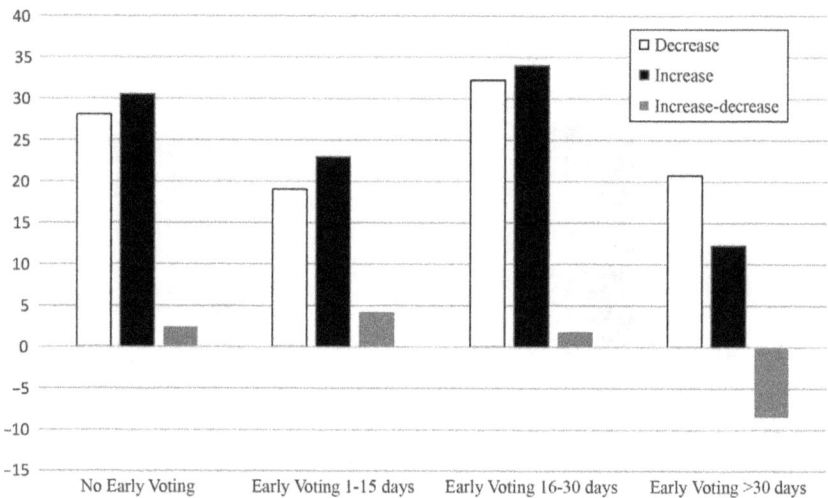

Figure 3.11   Revenue and Early Voting. Author.

and more than thirty days) when there is a decrease in expenditures but in two other categories (no early voting and early voting from sixteen to thirty days) when there are increases in expenditures. This leads to a rejection of Hypotheses 1 and 2. There is an odd and surprising increase in use of early voting more than thirty days among states with a decrease in revenue (figure 3.11). This also leads to a rejection of Hypothesis 2 but it could be that in those states that have more than thirty days of early voting, that this voting

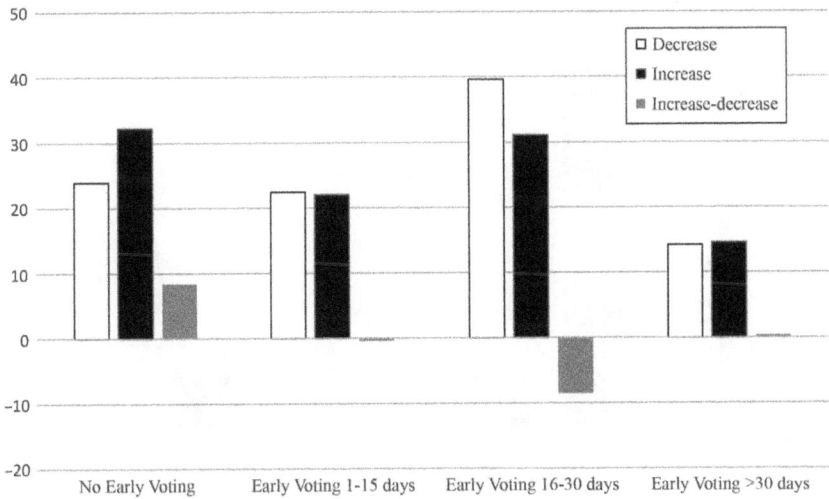

Figure 3.12   GDP and Early Voting. Author.

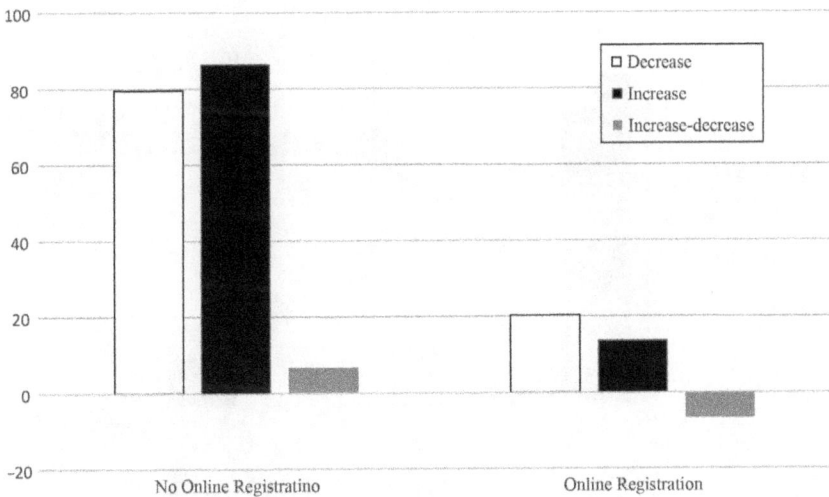

Figure 3.13   Expenditure and Online Registration. Author.

is held in clerks' offices that would be otherwise open and does not lead to any additional outlay of financial resources. Finally, when looking at GDP in figure 3.12, an increase in GDP leads to no early voting or an increase in early voting sixteen to thirty days before the election. This dichotomous relationship indicates that Hypothesis 2 should be rejected.

The analysis then turns to looking at online registration with the expectation of finding support for Hypothesis 3. In figures 3.12–3.15, online

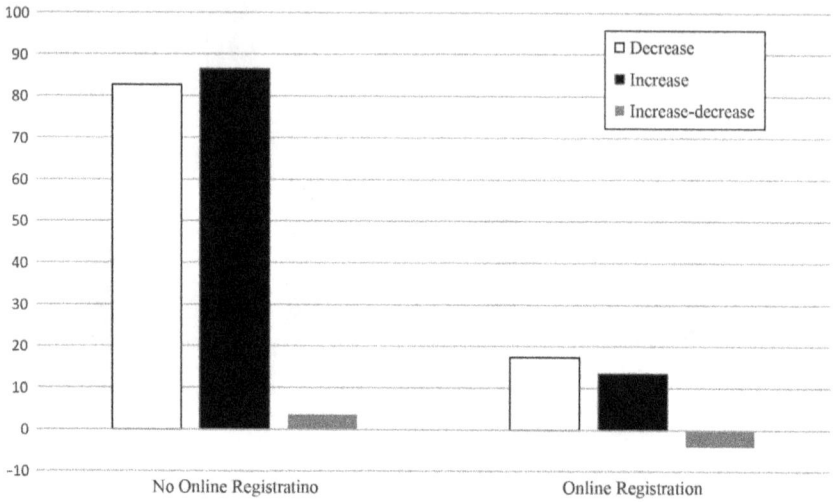

Figure 3.14 Revenue and Online Registration. Author.

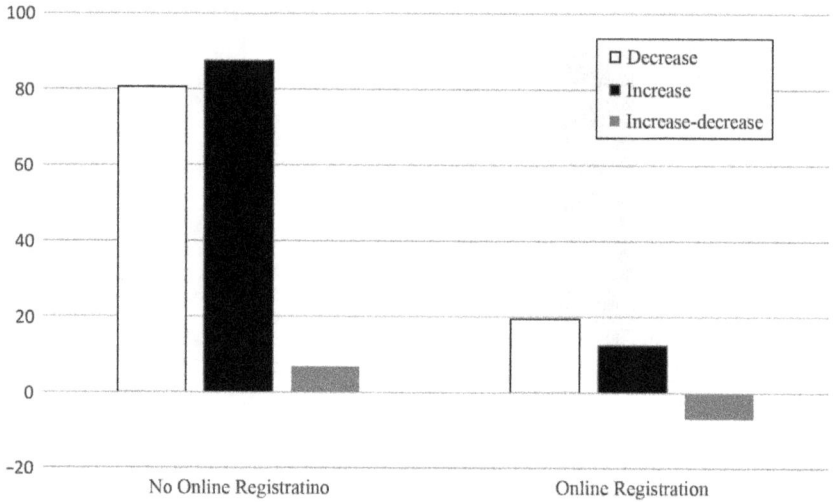

Figure 3.15 GDP and Online Registration. Author.

registration is used more when there is a decrease in expenditures, revenues, and GDP spending. This provides clear support for Hypothesis 3 as when expenditures and revenue decrease, states utilize cost-saving mechanisms (like online registration).

This analysis shows that the relationship between fiscal variables and voting laws is most clear and supportive of Hypotheses 1 and 2 when looking at voter identification laws (the most prominent of our voting law restrictions). Further, when there is a decrease in expenditures and revenue, states do turn to cost-saving strategies like online registration (providing support for Hypothesis 3). As a result of these findings, we establish a relationship and support our hypotheses. These are examined in a larger analysis in the next chapter in the context of larger data sets and with additional control variables.

NOTE

1. It should be noted the $290 billion appropriated was limited to some services—for example, state fiscal relief (Medicaid), state fiscal stabilization fund, education, economic recovery payments (TANF and child support), unemployment compensation, law enforcement, and infrastructure (highways, clean water, and public housing) (Congressional Budget Office 2009).

Chapter 4

Today

The Larger Economic Impact

While chapter 3 situates the impacts of the economic variables in a five-year period pre- and post-recession, it is important to determine if those effects continue to exist today. The analysis from here forward looks not only at this period but extends it to 2018 to see the current fiscal, partisan, and racial impacts.

HISTORICAL EXAMPLES OF FISCAL POLICIES

To situate this argument fully in the context of voting access, it is important to explore historical policies of voting restrictions and their connection to fiscal policies. Poll taxes were used to provide a source of revenue to the states but also an additional cost to the voting process. Poll taxes were a major source of income to the colonies. In fact, in Massachusetts, poll taxes made up one-third to one-half of their budget. Thus, there was some fiscal need behind enacting and continuing poll taxes (albeit its disproportional application in the post-Civil War in the South does not discount the racial overtones of the policy). Beyond the South, these fees were enacted in some northern and western states (including California, Connecticut, Maine, Massachusetts, Minnesota, New Hampshire, Ohio, Pennsylvania, Vermont, and Wisconsin) as well. Voters attempting to register would be asked to pay an additional fee before they could cast a ballot. If a voter was successful in paying the fee, additional fees could be assessed. These fees were also waived for low-income white voters but not for African Americans.

To demonstrate the fiscal connection of poll taxes beyond the exchange of money it is important to explore several court cases on the topic. In 1937, a lawsuit filed by a white man in Georgia alleged that the poll taxes violated the

Fourteenth and Nineteenth Amendments as he was required to pay a tax, and women who did not register to vote did not. In *Breedlove v. Suttles* (1932) the Supreme Court rejected claims arguing that the poll tax was a legitimate method for raising revenue for the state *Breedlove v. Suttles, 302 U.S. 277 (1937)*. The Twenty-Fourth Amendment was passed in 1964 to prohibit the use of a fee for voting in federal elections. Five states (Alabama, Arkansas, Mississippi, Texas, and Virginia) continued to use these fees at the state level until the Supreme Court declared them unconstitutional. As justification by the court for the use of poll taxes illustrates, economic influences are no stranger to limitations in government spending and especially when they apply to voting restrictions. Arguably, poll taxes were eliminated in 1964; however, a new Florida law in 2018 required felons to pay back court costs prior to being allowed to vote—often a fee of thousands of dollars (Madani 2019). Additionally, the requirement of voter identification has also been argued, because of the financial burden it can place on voters to purchase this identification.

Thus, the plan of this book is to explore voting access and state fiscal environments using the various data available on electoral administration. We expand the explanations of electoral administration and voting access policy and the motivations of the Republican Party in engaging in policy changes that limit voter access. Our core point is that without an acknowledgment of the role that Fiscal Conservatives continue to have in the ideological makeup of the Republican Party, the policy mechanisms they adopt in regard to changes to voting administration policy will likely be incomplete. The complexity that is the modern Republican Party will be clarified and, thus, leave our understanding of how these restrictions on voting access gain policy traction and ultimately become the adopted policy.

A series of analyses were run to investigate the aforementioned hypotheses. The first among these was an OLS regression of an election spending proxy on state expenditures, state revenues, and a number of control variables that were discussed in the previous chapter. As this ratio increased, states could be presumed to be spending less on elections, as the polling places were becoming more crowded and vice versa. Because this data relied on the Election Administration and Voting Survey, the analysis was restricted to election years from 2004 to 2016. While it may appear concerning to include expenditure and revenue in the same model, there was very little correlation between the two.

We also utilize several control variables to account for differing demographic, geographic, and economic realities facing states, which might account for the restrictiveness of their voting policies. Population is one of these, collected from the same sources as the race data. Using the raw population statistics, population density is calculated based on the 2010 land area estimates produced by the US Census Bureau (2010). State GDP data is derived from the US Bureau of Economic Analysis, and while not directly in the analyses, it is subsequently used to produce two different variables. The first of these is GDP per capita, and the second of these is state general expenditure as a percentage of GDP. GDP per capita is controlled for in the analysis as a predictor of the relative ability of states to maintain expensive (but expansionary) voting policies, like early voting, while the latter term accounted for the differing relative levels of expenditures between states. Exogenous regional differences are accounted for with the inclusion of a "west" and "south" binary term coded according to the regional definitions offered by the US Census Bureau Geography Program (n.d.). These regions were chosen specifically because of their connection to voting rights. The South has a long history of voter suppression and western states are known for advances in voting access (e.g., vote by mail). Finally, we included a year count variable starting with 1 = 2000. It is included to capture natural policy drift and take care of some early autocorrelation issues.

A few final general notes on the data collected. First, Alaska and Nebraska are universally excluded from the analyses. We did not include Nebraska because of the partisan nature of our analysis and their unicameral nonpartisan legislature would necessarily remove them from the partisan analysis regardless. Alaska was not included because of its economic eccentricities that would make it an outlier in the results consistent with the literature. We tested for collinearity issues among the control variables, even those that at a glance might appear to be a concern (such as the combination between a GDP per capita term and a spending percent of GDP term) and found no such issues exist in our data. On a final note, a number of interactions between the three sets of explanatory variables are featured in the analyses in chapters 5 and 6 to contribute to our larger theoretical argument. These are present to observe the mediating effects that the variables had upon one another.

We examined six dependent variables in our analysis. The first dependent variable is the ratio of registered voters to polling places. This is intended as a proxy for election spending, as the costly establishment of physical polling places is reasoned to reflect the general level of fiscal commitment to elections. The ratio is derived from the US Election Assistance Commission's Election and Administration Voting Survey (2019). As a result of depending on this survey, the registered voters to polling places term is restricted to election years from 2004 to 2016. Furthermore, due to incomplete responses given by state officials in some years, only 298 of the expected 336 observations (around 88 percent) had usable values. Luckily, non-reporting of this type is not a systematic issue excluding some states but varies from survey to survey. Mail-ballot-only states are excluded from this measure though, as while they did report statistics for the handful of polling places, they obviously did not have or need the same voting infrastructure and produced ratios of over 10,000 voters per polling place. This provides a baseline to compare the differences in voter identification laws.

Table 4.1 provides the descriptive statistics of the variables utilized in this analysis.

Using all of the collected data, a series of OLS regressions, binary logistic regressions, and ordinal regressions are presented in the following pages and chapters. The analyses in each chapter from here take a stepwise approach, initially testing a heavily restricted model only including the main terms of interest and then building up to a more robust conclusion to better present a picture of the relationships between variables. For the ordinal models specifically, there is one additional issue to address. All such analyses had significant results for a test of parallel lines, raising some concerns about the assumption of proportional odds. The test is famously biased toward significance, however, and the strong theoretical purposes for using an ordinal approach (namely getting at an underlying continuous "voting restrictiveness" term) justified the use of such models.

Looking at table 4.2, we examine the significant relationship between the percentage of a state's GDP that was expended and the election spending

Table 4.1   Descriptive Statistics

	Minimum	Maximum	Mean	Std. Deviation	N
TR per PP	551.28	3268.90	1597.55	612.583	298
Voter ID	1	5	1.927	1.241	864
Early Voting	0	3	1.251	1.043	864
Permanent Absentee	0	2	.401	.660	864
Online Registration	0	1	.222	.416	864
No Excuse	0	1	.514	.500	864
Revenue Percent Change	−24.83	27.23	2.170	4.457	816
Expenditure Percent Change	−7.84	34.27	4.479	4.319	816
GDP per Capita (thousands)	30.56	78.08	48.551	9.108	864
Spending Percent of GDP	4.77	20.70	9.946	2.662	864
Population (Millions)	.49	39.40	6.280	6.782	864
Population Density (Tens/sq mile)	.51	120.86	20.071	26.052	864
West	0	1	.2500	.4333	864
South	0	1	.3333	.4717	864
Year	1	18	9.500	5.1911	864

Source: Author.

Table 4.2   OLS Regression: Registered Voters per Polling Place and Economic Variables

	Model 1+	Model 2
Revenue Percent Change	−1.797	3.065
	(8.454)	(7.787)
Expenditure Percent Change	3.868	7.159
	(9.468)	(8.429)
GDP per Capita (thousands)		4.203
		(4.235)
Spending per GDP		−73.319**
		(15.098)
Population (millions)		−4.987
		(4.794)
Population Density (10 sq/mile		7.012**
		(1.382)
Year		107.296**
		(18.348)
West		230.501**
		(85.499)
South		70.103
		(73.836)
Constant	1584.508**	1504.353**
	(49.208)	(287.716)
Obs	298	298
R2	−.006	.254
F	.083	12.222**

Source: Author.
**$p<.01$ + autocorrelation evident. Standard errors provided in brackets.

proxy. At least indirectly, the negative relationship between these two variables provided some confidence in the use of the registered voters per polling place as a proxy, as it is intuitive that as the relative scope of state expenditures decreased, spending on elections would also decrease. Another major aspect to note in table 4.2 is the lack of evidence for the Hypothesis 1. Neither of the two fiscal variables have a significant impact on the ratio between registered voters per polling places in either model. It is worth mentioning that this was the case even when the variables were coded as a percentage change, percentage decline, or as a binary decline/no decline variable. Even the inclusion of lags to capture delayed effects had no influence on the results. Instead, the election spending proxy was primarily explained by the aforementioned control variables: GDP per capita, population density, a "west" regional indicator, and the year variable. Additionally, the inclusion of the year term was sufficient to remedy the initial issues with autocorrelation.

Table 4.3 is an ordinal regression of the previously discussed voting identification scale on the same explanatory variables. In table 4.3, there is no evidence for Hypothesis 3b's prediction that a decrease in state revenue would increase the probability of enacted voting restrictions in either model. There was some support for Hypothesis 1 in Model 1 with a decrease in

Table 4.3 Ordinal Regression: Voting ID Scale and Economic Variables

	Model 1	Model 2
Revenue Percent Change	−.013 (0.17)	−.021 (.018)
Expenditure Percent Change	−.075** (.018)	−025 (020)
GDP per Capita (thousands)		−.031** (.010)
Spending per GDP		−.341** (0.39)
Population (millions)		−.016 (0.12)
Population Density (10 sq/mile)		−.013** (.010)
West		−.342 (.195)
South		.914** (.168)
Year		.233** (.020)
Obs	816	816
Cox and Snell	.031	.265
Chi-Square	25.933**	251.32**

Source: Author.
Goodness of Fit—Nonsignificant | Test of Parallel Lines—Significant; **p* value <.01. Standard error in brackets.

Table 4.4 Ordinal Regression: Early Voting Scale and Economic Variables

	Model 1	Model 2
Revenue Percent Change	.009 (.016)	.004 (.016)
Expenditure Percent Change	.002 (.016)	.013 (.018)
GDP per Capita (thousands)		−.014 (.010)
Spending per GDP		.006 (.033)
Population (millions)		.041** (.010)
Population Density (tens sq/mile)		−.017** (.003)
West		.072 (.174)
South		−1.042** (.163)
Year		.036** (.017)
Obs	816	816
Cox and Snell	.001	.129
Chi-Square	.493	112.859**

Source: Author.
**p* value <.01. Standard error in brackets.
Model 1: Goodness of Fit—Nonsignificant | Test of Parallel Lines—Nonsignificant.
Model 2: Goodness of Fit—Significant | Test of Parallel Lines—Significant.

expenditures but this is no longer significant when adding the controls in Model 2. Beyond the key dependent variables, states that were wealthier spent a larger portion of their GDP, and denser populations had a lower probability of moving toward more restrictive voting policies. Finally, Southern states were the most likely to adopt such changes, and the natural course of policy diffusion made states progressively more likely to adopt restrictive policies as time went on. This is unsurprising given the proliferation of voter identification laws in the South post-*Shelby*.

Table 4.4 is an ordinal regression of the early voting scale (defined by its election periods) on the same variables as included in tables 4.1 and 4.2. While

Table 4.5   Binary Logistic Regression: Online Registration and Economic Variables

	Model 1	Model 2
Revenue Percent Change	.022 (.021)	.015 (.028)
Expenditure Percent Change	−.068** (.023)	.003 (.030)
GDP per Capita (thousands)		.011 (.014)
Spending per GDP		−.176** (.053)
Population (millions)		.001 (.017)
Population Density (tens sq/mile)		.003 (.005)
West		2.124** (.316)
South		.467 (.284)
Year		.491** (.040)
Constant	−.938** (.116)	−6.740** (1.051)
Obs	816	816
Cox and Snell	.011	.363
Chi-Square	9.327**	367.849**

Source: Author.
**p value <.01. Standard error in brackets.

Model 1 provides no significant findings, Model 2 demonstrates that only our control variables are significant. Neither revenue nor expenditures have any significant effect, again failing to meet the expectation of Hypotheses 1 and 2.

Table 4.5 is a binary logistic regression of online registration on the economic variables and the control terms. This provides a test of Hypothesis 3, as the expectation would be to see a significant negative coefficient for the revenue percent change variable (showing that as revenue decreased the probability of enacting online registration increased). This result makes sense, as online registration is a cost-saving activity (after the initial set up of the system) and is cheaper to maintain than paper records that require personnel to input. As seen in table 4.5, the revenue term was not significant and thus failed to meet this expectation. Something interesting to observe from these results, however, is that the relationship between relative state spending and the enactment of online registration was negative. In other words, state governments with greater relative funds under their control were less likely to enact online registration—a finding in line with the spirit of Hypothesis 3 albeit looking at the control variables, and not the key independent variables.

Following the online registration analysis is another ordinal regression evaluating the enactment of permanent absentee lists. In table 4.6, neither of the fiscal variables has a significant effect on the odds of adopting such policy. Thus, in this analysis there is no evidence of a link between fiscal realities and policy changes, proving the null of Hypotheses 1 and 2. The results make it apparent that permanent absentee lists are the preferred policy of wealthier, well-funded, and more populous states in general, as well as western states specifically. Also of some interest was nonsignificance of the

Table 4.6 Ordinal Regression: Permanent Absentee Scale and Economic Variables

	Model 1	Model 2
Revenue Percent Change	.008 (019)	.008 (.019)
Expenditure Percent Change	−.026 (.020)	−.041 (.021)
GDP per Capita (thousands)		.028** (.011)
Spending per GDP		.233** (.039)
Population (millions)		.063** (.012)
Population Density (tens sq/mile)		.014** (.003)
West		1.717** (.213)
South		−.391 (.217)
Year		−.016 (.021)
Obs	816	816
Cox and Snell	.002	.187
Chi-Square	1.741	168.931**

Source: Author.
**p value <.01. Standard error in brackets.
Model 1: Goodness of Fit—Nonsignificant | Test of Parallel Lines—Nonsignificant.
Model 2: Goodness of Fit—Nonsignificant | Test of Parallel Lines—Significant.

Table 4.7 Binary Logistic Regression: No-Excuse Absentee and Economic Variables

	Model 1	Model 2
Revenue Percent Change	.026 (.018)	.019 (.021)
Expenditure Percent Change	.001 (.018)	.016 (.023)
GDP per Capita (thousands)		−.027** (.013)
Spending per GDP		−.065 (.043)
Population (millions)		−.006 (.014)
Population Density (tens sq/mile)		−.013** (.004)
West		2.143** (.279)
South		−1.031** (.193)
Year		.091** (.023)
Constant	.024 (.101)	1.261 (.797)
Obs	816	816
Cox and Snell	.003	.258
Chi-Square	2.779	243.970**

Source: Author.
**p value <.01. Standard error in brackets.

year variable, unique among the analyses of this chapter, which suggested that permanent absentee voting lists are not naturally drifting toward adoption beyond the discussed state characteristics. The significance and direction of western states is unsurprising, as many have adopted systems to make election participation easier.

Finally, table 4.7 is a regression analysis of no-excuse absentee voting policy. We expect to find support for Hypothesis 3 and 3b; however, the economic coefficients of interest are not significant. As a result of this analysis, we can propose a general profile of a state likely to enact no-excuse absentee voting. Such a state was less dense and less wealthy, which, while not a key explanatory independent variable, was nonetheless, noteworthy. Western states are significantly more likely to adopt such policies and Southern states are significantly less likely to adopt no-excuse absentee voting.

CONCLUSION

We began our exploration of voting access restrictions believing that fiscal stress would be a strong predictor of the likelihood of the adoption, especially when the expansion would be clearly linked to increased costs. And while we do find some evidence that the increased costs are viewed as potential threat, they are not the dominant concerns that drive the policy adoption. Instead of finding support for our key variables, our analysis shows that Hypotheses 1 and 2 have no significant findings beyond the initial findings in chapter 3. Budgets and revenue do not drive adoption of these policies. As such, the only variable of economic significance is the control variable of GDP per capita. This finding demonstrates that the general wealth of a state influences the adoption of these policies, to provide some minor support for Hypothesis 3 when it comes to online registration and permanent absentee status.

Thus, we find a more nuanced story emerging, one where our threat theory is active across a number of potential explanations, and one where with policy door open to any number of potential approaches to attempt to mitigate the threat response of voters, elected officials are free to rely on a variety of reason for adopting the voter access restrictions, such as fiscal conservatism in wake of a recession. But in actuality, there is limited causality of economic factors on adopting more restrictive policies.

Chapter 5

Partisan Influences

As I noted in the beginning of this book, I come from the general tradition of fiscal conservatism and libertarianism. It is from that perspective that I find my partisan identity and what contributed to some of the analysis of this book. While the premise of this book was to look at economic factors in voting access changes, economics works in concert with many other factors, and as such, it is critical to examine partisanship. Furthermore, you cannot explore economic influences on policy without partisanship—especially when invoking fiscal conservatism. Thus, in light of the previous chapter's findings, we explore partisanship in this chapter as an explanation of the recent voting restrictions. There are concrete reasons to start with partisanship. The literature tells us that partisanship plays a significant role in policy development. There is a historical norm of party and as a behavioralist, there is a clear effect of partisanship on everything from budgeting to policy enactment. In fact, to ignore partisanship would limit the authority of this book and seemingly is the logical next step in the examination of voting restrictions.

When each party comes to power, there is always some jockeying for continued partisan control. This means changes in executive leadership, policy changes, and even some changes in spending patterns. Thus, the role that partisanship plays in voting regulations is not unexamined. Typically, the literature has focused on the impact of election rules on party rather than its converse: the role of parties on election laws (Grofman and Lijphart 1986; Kimball, Kropf, and Battles 2006; Hicks et al. 2015). Some literature does discuss the role that partisan decisions play in terms of redistricting (e.g., Abramowitz 1983; Cain and Campagna 1987; Niemi and Abramowitz 1994; Squire 1985; Cain 1985). Knowing the extent to which partisanship shapes redistricting election laws can be extrapolated to understanding the role that partisanship has on election laws (particularly *Rucho v. Common Cause* 2019[1]).

Within the coalition of factions that make up the modern Republican Party, two groups have had substantial sway over the policy orientation of the party and while not currently dominant in the leadership of the party, still remain crucial to the success of the party. The first is the Libertarian segment of the party, which has seen substantial policy influence in fiscal, tax, and spending policy with their focus on reducing the size of government and limiting the areas in which it operates. The Libertarians have long been closely aligned with the larger and considerably more influential group of Fiscal Conservatives that, until the rise of the religious right in the mid-1980s, had been the dominant faction of the Republican Party. Despite the weakening of this group across the last three decades, this coalition, particularly on fiscal and economic policy matters, has remained an important part of the Republican coalition that must be mollified, and their policy preference addressed. Thus, our larger argument about the role of fiscal conservatism goes hand in hand with the partisanship.

Central to the Republican coalition are the Fiscal Conservatives and Libertarians we described earlier, with their deeply skeptical orientation toward government spending, increases in government services, and other actions that are likely to increase taxes. They exist in this coalition with a variety of other interests including Christian conservatives, war hawks, neo-cons, the populist Tea Party, and the much-discussed Alt Right with their nativist leanings toward white supremacy. The structure of the American electoral system and its resulting two-party system requires these disparate interests to coexist inside the party in the search for electoral wins. As a result, policy outcomes are often born of multiple causes as the coalition lurches toward a policy position. Because of the nature of the coalition that is the modern Republican Party, we propose that in the policy formulation process, fiscal conservatism is vital to the larger Republican coalition. Fiscal motivations and explanations, although perhaps as secondary influences, serve to bring Fiscal Conservatives along with the preferred policy outcome of other members of the Republican coalition.

The role of partisanship in policymaking is of particular importance to the consideration of voter access policies. Unquestionably, partisanship plays a role in the legislature (Hibbings and Theiss-Morse 1995, 2002) and the legislation passed. There are those who believe that partisanship drives policy (Aldrich 1995; Cox and McCubbins 1993, 2005) and those that believe that majoritarian preferences drive the policies (Brady and Volden 1998; Krehbiel 1993, 1998). Research indicates that at the state level, where voting laws are made, ideological preferences dominate over all other variables as the cause of specific policies (Erikson, Wright, and McIver 1993). The policies passed by different parties are also part of issue ownership (Petrocik 1996); and that these issue preferences are reflective in the spending of each party. There also appears to be a partisan impact on state spending and taxes (Dawson and Robinson 1963). While there tends to be marginal higher overall spending by those on the left than those on the right (Blais, Blake, and Dion 1993), the choice of where to focus funding is primarily a partisan decision. Other literature suggests that on the aggregate, partisanship does not play a role on policy decisions at the states level (Dawson and Robinson 1963; Dye 1996; Lewis-Beck 1977; Hwang and Gray 1991). The literature also indicates a pattern of partisanship is not universal, rather influences over specific policy areas: trade (Milner and Judkins 2004; Dutt and Mitra 2005) and welfare (Dawson and Robinson 1963; Barrilleaux and Miller 1988; Buchanan, Cappelleri, and Ohsfeldt 1991; Garand and Hendick 1991; Marquette and Hinckley 1981; Peterson and Rom 1990; Plotnick and Winters 1990). Thus, one cannot explore economics without partisan interactions in policymaking.

The more partisanship is explored in the data and the role of threats in policymaking, the more it became clear that exploring the factions of the Republican Party is an important step in understanding the process of voting access restrictions becoming law. As such, a brief exploration of the factions and how those factions have come to coexist in the modern Republican Party is an important part of the story. This story is likely not unique to the modern Republican coalitions but instead represents periods of turmoil and evolution within the party that have been ongoing at least since the Clinton administration.

PARTY FACTIONS

We can readily identify at least four distinct and substantial parts of the coalition that exist in the modern Republican Party. While these are the most prominent, there may be as many as several dozen additionally identifiable groups within the party. However, these four are critical to the coalition and are those most likely to impact the voter access discussion.

We identify the following key groups: (1) Moral Conservatives and the Religious Right, (2) Fiscal Conservatives and Traditional Republicans, (3) The Tea Party and Neo-Populists, and (4) the Alt Right Nativist Coalition. We also suggest a fifth group (Libertarians) with strong feelings on these issues but who represent only a small part of the modern Republican Party. Please note that Libertarian or Libertarian-leaning Republicans often have strong overlap with the Fiscal Conservatives. Despite being identifiable, we have no reason to predict that this group differs from the Fiscal Conservatives' preferences on policy issue surrounding voter access.

These factions represent a wide and disparate swath of conservatism and conservative thinking. Thus, by bringing the groups together there are consequences for the wider policy positions taken by the party and these positions may be compromise positions or they may represent the domination of one group over the others in the final policy decision. An example of this domination is readily taken from the most recent presidential elections, which resulted in the election of a Republican president. In both the George W. Bush and Donald J. Trump elections, the Tea Party/populist members of the coalition have seen their policy preferences dominate both the Fiscal Conservatives and Moral Conservatives either by changes in policy orientation or by knocking preferred issues from the party's agenda.

Unfortunately, there has developed a notion of monolithic party preference that little resembles the plurality of policy preferences that exist among the various groups that make up the current Republican Party. Similarly monolithic explanations and understandings of the Republican (and Democratic) Party have become the default position with little attention paid to how the internal dynamics of the party impact the policy positions that rise to the top of the policy agenda. In this chapter, we first review each of the members of the coalition and then discuss how the existence of the coalition and the manner in which the members engage in the political process to gain traction for their preferred policy outcome.

Easily the most recognizable and arguably the faction whose policy preferences are most ascendant are those of the neo-populist or Tea Party conservatives. The Tea Party and the Trump-style populists that followed them emerged in the mid- to late-2000s in response to growing dissatisfaction both with the economic conditions of the Great Recession. This is certainly not an uncommon story in the history of either party but this emergence represented something meaningfully different (see: Skocpol and Williamson 2016; Hoschschild 2018; Arceneaux and Nicholson 2012). The rhetoric of the inherent morality and rightness of the common man became the mantra first of the Tea Party with its ideation on Joe the Plumber who rose into the national consciousness during a televised debate with a decidedly plain-spoken approach, and by ultimately asking the question, *What about me and those like me?* At the time of the Tea Party's rise in the Republican Party, its members in Congress had pushed for an active bailout of large banks. These banks found themselves insolvent largely due to their investment in subprime mortgages resulting in a subsequent crisis, leaving what had long been considered among the safest parts of the investment economy—housing mortgages—in shambles. As the bailout progressed through Congress, those who were directly impacted by the wave of foreclosures and the accompanying near-freezing of the credit market increasingly found themselves with few options to continue the lifestyle that both easy credit and never-ending increases in home prices had allowed through the 1990s and early 2000s.

In response to these newfound economic threats and the new reality of greatly reduced economic opportunity, we see the mobilization of voters who would first be the Tea Party voters, and later at the core of the Trump populist voters. These voters are a group of white, lower-middle-class, blue-collar, largely suburban, and rural rust belt voters who would respond to perceived threats first after the election of Barack Obama. They further felt further threatened from the bank bailout and other attempts to remedy the 2008 financial crisis that focused on "Wall Street" rather than "Main Street." There were increased demands for policies from these voters to mitigate the economic threats they perceived and a system they believed was "rigged" against their success.

The 2010 election would be the first election with this new populist coalition then called the Tea Party, active and dominating in the electoral math. Even such conservative stalwarts as US senator for Utah Robert Bennett would be replaced in an attempt to push the Republican Party toward the populist demands of the Tea Party. Senator Bennett is emblematic of the rise of the Tea Party populists and their impact on the Republican Party. Bennett is clearly a member of the fiscal conservative part of the Republican coalition and his voting record repeatedly led him to be ranked as the most or second-most conservative member of the Republican Senate Caucus. However, his fiscal conservatism and a pragmatic approach to compromise were quickly viewed as a being "liberal" or during this period and for this new populism, an ally of President Obama or the big banks. Utah's other senator would quickly learn the lesson, and quickly adopted much of the Tea Party populist's agenda as his own. This movement would continue through the remainder of the Obama administration and would be primed for Donald Trump to stoke in the months and years leading up to the 2016 election. Indeed their sense of alienation, abandonment, and sense of general malaise would largely calcify during the final years of the Obama administration often at the urging of the new group of politicians that had swept into power. Obama would come to represent the great other that was the source of their sense of being threatened. This group of white, lower-middle-class, generally blue-collar, rural, and suburban voters would quickly articulate the threat they were feeling socially and economically, and politicians quickly began to use that threat to match policy positions that would at least seemingly have the potential to mitigate the threat.

Thus with the strength of this segment of the party well-established, the policy environment within the Republican Party shifted to include the reality that this newly activated populist segment both could and would oust those they viewed as being unwilling to address their issues. The primary and in many ways the only policy area of significance is the perception of being continually under threat. First, economically, and as other policy entrepreneurs recognized the potential power of this group within the coalition from the impact of immigrant labor, over reaching federal government, liberals, and perhaps most disturbingly and likely at the root of our examination of the expansion of voting rights restrictions, threat from those viewed as other especially nonwhite racial and ethnic groups.

Where do the attempts to mitigate the threats come from? Relatively few have emerged from populist movement itself, and indeed this is consistent with many populist uprisings; they are too easily captured by charismatic leaders, or other policy entrepreneurs. Here enters Donald Trump, an unlikely, if perennial, candidate starting in at least 2000. Trump, like many who end up at the head of populist movements, has a clear charisma and a relatively simple message. For Trump, this message quickly became "Make America Great Again" and few slogans could better capture the dissatisfaction of this group, this sense of pining for something lost and the promise of something better. The slogan which in its very construction seems to acknowledge that at some point in the past. Thing had been better, primed these populists to seek out those that they could then identify as having contributed to the slide of American greatness, and ultimately the source of threat. Often populist movements simply become reflections of the preferences of the charismatic leader, but in this case the source of preferences emerge largely from the other members of the Republican coalition and have become part and parcel of the ongoing demands articulated by the populist swell. This unique arrangement, where the populist swell seems to be focused primarily on an existential threat, has quickly been co-opted by other members of the coalition and grafted on the populist wave.

Among the first groups to identify the opportunity for policy entrepreneurship using the populist movement inside the Republican Party were the Moral Conservatives, who through the 1980s were the group most clearly identified as one of the cleavages within the broader Republican Party. The Moral Conservatives are concerned with "values." Moral conservative is the name given to a relatively wide group of interests that range from traditionalists to the religious right most associated with the 1980s. These groups largely coalesced into a single faction in the 1990s and have come to identify with two major policy initiatives. The hallmark of these two initiatives is that they engage moral conservative voters on purely moral grounds, and policy grounds or explanations become secondary as they attempt to merge them into the wider Republican Party platform. This connects with the Southern Strategy, which was then co-opted into a moral issue to continue to engage Southern Democrats and the religious right. Abortion is a hallmark of this strategy and a primary policy issue since *Roe v. Wade* legalized abortion nationwide. A second moral issue that was able to mobilize voters in the early 2000s was opposition to gay marriage. For this group, both of these issues identify as moral imperatives against which to rally the fight. These issues also provide an arena for Moral Conservatives to focus and exert the most influence on the preferences of the new populist wave.

In the search for ways to mitigate the existential threat, the new populism has focused on the Moral Conservatives presented a way to maintain the status quo and to prevent wholesale change that has been widely adopted among those we would identify as the Tea Party or neo-populists, that is, the selection of conservative judges, especially judges who are more likely to invalidate both *Roe v. Wade* and *Obergefell v. Hodges*, and to hold a hard line on social change implemented through courts. This mantra for conservative judges has quickly become a key part of both President Trump's agenda with two Supreme Court confirmations as of mid-2019. Both Brett Kavanaugh and especially Neil Gorsuch match both the desires of Moral Conservatives and those that have grafted on to the notion of conservative judges as a way to mitigate the fear resulting from cultural shifts. Kavanaugh's confirmation is of particular importance as he replaces Anthony Kennedy who was the key swing vote and caused substantial frustration for the Moral Conservatives. Kennedy was also viewed as the root cause of the legalization of gay marriage and the continued legalization of abortion. It remains to be seen if this replacement moves the court on either of these core issues, but the move toward conservative justices as part of the populist policy agenda in the current era is of particular importance in the story that surrounds access to voting. Without this focus on and demand for relatively hardcore conservative jurisprudence, it is unlikely that voting access limitations could have taken hold. The recent cases in 2019 regarding partisan gerrymandering add confirmation to this weariness in the court.

The third group on the coalition that has attempted to graft their policy preferences onto the ascendant populism are Fiscal Conservatives, and their close allies, the Libertarian Republicans. This group which harbors deep concern about the cost of government, and in the case of the Libertarians, the scope of government action, has, like the Moral Conservatives, attempted to attach their policy agenda to the populist rise with varying degrees of success. A deep skepticism of Washington and the cost of social welfare programs have emerged as one of the key populist policy concerns. This group likewise opposes runaway democracy and decides to implement new social programs based on future tax increases or deficit spending and has categorized overspending and the national debt as one of the gravest threats that public policy should address.

This focus on cost and size of government alongside the desire of the moral conservative for the status quo, and focus on conservative judges along with the ascendant populism, created an opening for the most nefarious of the Republican coalition members, indeed one the Republican Party itself has largely excommunicated, and yet, it remains an active player in conservative politics. The Alt Right and its explicitly racialized vision of public policy have focused on the perceived lost dominance of white control. The Alt Right is often presented through the lens not of racism but of reverence for Western culture, or white pride. Regardless of how it is portrayed, the explicit racialization of their policy issues can be clearly associated with some substantial level of racial animus. This view of policy through a racial lens, often with the express purpose of counteracting the increasing influence and power of minority groups, has been presented to the new populists as one of the sources of threat to their economic, social, and overall well-being. The Republican coalition that had largely been settled with Fiscal and Moral Conservatives vying for dominance has been upset by the emergence of the Alt Right and the new populists. What had been settled both in electoral politics and in policy preferences is largely because the two groups had little overlap in the issues. What issues they viewed as most important has now been disrupted, by a group largely responding to perceived threats that activated their entrance into Republican Party politics.

While we view the policy preferences of the new "Trump" populists as largely having been focused on the existential sense of threat carefully cultivated and largely co-opted by other members of the Republican coalition, these "Trump" populists articulate policy preferences that are the not the preferences of others members of the coalition, and are in fact in direct conflict with the Fiscal Conservatives. These new populists have consistently called for the elimination of free trade agreements, including the North American Free Trade Agreement that they view as having decimated their economic prospects, and the Trans-Pacific Partnership, which they believed would increase economic pressures on manufacturing and the industries these groups perceive as essential for their well-being. Although there is some evidence to suggest that the manufacturing sector is not, in fact, the dominant area of employment for many of the new populists. They further have pushed for increased tariffs on foreign manufactured goods, under the belief that by increasing the costs of foreign-made products will mitigate the economic threat.

As we have argued throughout the first chapters of this book, we view threat theory and the response of individual citizens as being at the root of most of the policy preferences that have come to dominate the Republican coalition as the new populists have risen in both size and importance. Our understanding of the existential threat and the response of citizens, and ultimately how elected officials have responded, was used to rebalance the coalition (since 2008, the rise of the Tea Party and the subsequent emergence of the Trump populists) to push forward their own policy preferences. The 2016 election was particularly emblematic of the way in which the coalition used the sense of existential threat, as the basis for public policy, an issue that by most measures of policy salience should not have come to dominate the election. Instead of more traditional Republican issues such as national defense, limiting spending, and even abortion or gay rights, the dominant issue pushed by Republican candidates, and especially by Donald Trump, was the threat posed by immigration.

The new populists quickly identified with the message that the Trump campaign had focused and refined to respond to the existential threat that was plaguing many of the white rural and suburban voters who despite an improving economy overall felt left behind and continued to feel threatened. Trump, and over time, other members of the Republican coalition gave form to the source of the treat. Immigrants, especially illegal immigrants, became that face. The rhetoric of the Trump campaign and eventually the policies he would implement following his election, have quickly and deliberately focused on the notion that immigration is risk to not just the economic circumstance of this group but also as a threat to security. This threat to security was supported by claims about the propensity of immigrants to commit crime, especially violent crime, and even terrorism. Beyond these two key claims, a general claim about the diminished nature of America and the American dream became the focus. Thus, policy suggestions were focused mostly on how to return a sense of lost greatness. While the new populists are clearly the most recent group to respond primarily to fear, as we have already identified, the Tea Party had similar roots focused in similar areas to those that deviated from the perceived status quo of American culture, economics, or who differed in preferences or culture from those who felt threatened.

We view voter access restrictions as largely emerging from this policy environment, first where the Tea Party identified an existential threat and rallied, and pushed for reforms including reforms to the Democratic process to limit changes to the electorate and resulting public policy, and then evolved into the new populists that identified difference as threat, especially from immigrants. The policy response then incorporated both the racialized views of the Alt Right, the concern for costs of the fiscal conservative, alongside a strong preference for a status quo culture rooted in the past of the Moral Conservatives. Taken together the policy of limited immigration, economic isolation, cultural conservatism, and limits on access to the ballot box became policy outcomes that suddenly gained traction both inside the party and ultimately in Republican state legislatures across the country.

A final source of concern similarly emerged as the new populist gained traction in the electoral process, as "constitutional conservatives" (their own term and not one that we would necessarily agree with), a descriptor for either their policy views or their core beliefs. Similarly, this group captured the threat narrative and began to speak about the threat that expanded ballot access posed to the constitutional order, and the sanctity of the electoral process. This group, while certainly active prior to the emergence of the Tea Party and the new populists, was able to seize on the rhetoric of threat that the new populists and the evolving Republican coalition had adopted.

These constitutional conservatives began to cast their concern for changes to the political order; these were seen as a threat to the American experience. The result has rallied Republicans for reigning in activist judges, limiting the influence of direct democracy, and creating concern about the knowledge that some voters bring to the electoral process. They view access to the ballot box by those they view as least likely to be making rational informed decisions as posing some degree of threat. It is not surprising that they view as least likely to be able to make informed choices as the same groups least likely to agree with the conservative interpretation of the constitution and the policy prescriptions generally identified with the Republican coalition. This group expresses their opposition to making voting easier, or to putting obstacles to voting access in public policy, as concern for the democratic system (preserving the ballot box and eliminating fraud), constitutional order, and for good public policy. In this way, they echo much of the founders' concern over excess democracy and, in fact, claim these concerns as their basis. This, however, appears to be viewed through a strong ideological lens that leaves it open for manipulation, bias, and ultimately, to being used in league with those who articulate less than noble motivations.

Our view of this coalition of interests that the Republican Party has become, particularly with its focus on threat and attempts to mitigate that threat through public policy, leads us directly to the hypotheses we present later in this chapter. For public policy to emerge effectively in this coalition, particularly with the support of the new populists, it must address the existential sense of threat these Republicans articulate and are searching for ways to mitigate. Through this lens, many of the most controversial policies endorsed by the Republicans can be explained, despite there being far from universal agreement among party elites and members on the instrumental policy. Immigration limits, reductions to free trade, and (we believe) ultimately a limit on voter access are all best explained through this lens. The limits to voter access are a result of this same coalition. This coalition is therefore the explanation of how these policies develop—which share the most similarity with the limitations on voter access of the Jim Crow era and are radically different from the last third of the twentieth century's approach of near-universal expansion of voter access endorsed by both parties.

We find that as perceived threat increased among a growing part of the Republican Party's base, and as that base increasingly became populist in its worldview and began to demand policy response to the perceived threats, elected officials have responded from a desire to satisfy the increasingly influential and certainly vocal part of the party. They began to demonstrate an openness to policy options that had previously been untenable. The disruption of the neo-populists and their Tea Party predecessors created a political opening for those who view expanded voting access, and democracy as a source threat to economic development, cultural status quo, partisan dominance, and those with some degree of racial animus, to act. These actions attempt to mitigate the perceived threats and form the basis of our empirical exploration of the motivations behind these limits to voting access.

As we explore the motivations, our focus is on race and ethnicity, partisan protectionism, and concern for the costs, all of which are deeply rooted in a perception of threat, and the changing nature of the Republican coalition. Our vision is not one of traditional racialized politics, although race is clearly active. Likewise, our view is not just one of partisan protectionism where Republican legislatures are simply protecting Republican majorities, although this too is active. We find that while the costs of these changes in voter access are active in the policy discussion, they do not dominate the roots. We instead find evidence for a more nuanced story rooted in individual concerns about economics, cultural change, and a general feeling of existential threat, and brought to policy fruition from the changing coalition that is the Republican Party and the elected officials that emerge from it.

In this chapter, we explore how voter access limitations have been presented to this wing of the Republican Party. We argue how those explanations (while insufficient to explain the large-scale adoption of these restrictions, given the role of the threat hypothesis and its accompanying issues of race and ethnicity and the partisan protectionism) remain an important nuance to what could otherwise be dismissed as mere nativism, racism, or partisanship. To be clear, we find strong evidence for nativism, racism, and partisanship as a basis for these sorts of policies both now and in the past, but understanding the nuance of how these policies are sold intraparty provides important insight into how these sorts of policies come to dominate.

In the course of at least the last three elections, frustrations and divergent beliefs about the voting process (particularly about access to the process) have risen in saliency to the point where they have begun to take center stage in electoral process and even to dominate the rhetoric used by candidates. This discussion of the election administration and the resulting impacts represents one of the few times in American politics that discussions of process have become salient to the average citizen.

To situate the role of partisanship in voting barriers, we examine the historical role that partisanship has played in the limitation of voting rights.

DIFFERENT TYPES OF PARTISAN
ELECTORAL BARRIER POLICIES

Jim Crow laws are the foundation of historical discrimination in voting rights.[2] While many Jim Crow laws have racial overtones, some have very specific partisan connections as well (for both parties). This section examines the grandfather clause, felon disenfranchisement, and redistricting as a function of partisan electoral barriers.

The grandfather clause has a complex history in the United States rooted in the Deep South and starting in Louisiana. The Democratic Party won control of the state legislature in Louisiana in 1876 and implemented the grandfather clause in 1898 by including a provision that allowed illiterate and impoverished men to register only if their father or grandfathers had voted anywhere prior to January 1, 1867 (Riser 2010; Wormser n.d.). Further, the White's Only Primary had partisan overtones (the racial component of these laws will also be in the next chapter) by preventing voters from participating in the primary, and all but guaranteed that the winner of the Democratic primary would be uncontested in the general election. This protected the Democratic Party from external threats by limiting who could participate in the primary and guaranteed that the nominee would represent particular interests of the party faithful. While the White's Only Primary was struck down by the Supreme Court in *Nixon v. Herndon* (1927), Texas passed a subsequent law that allowed parties to determine who could participate in their primary. The Texas Democratic Party limited participation and party membership to white Democrats to circumvent *Nixon v. Herndon* and was upheld until *Terry v. Adams* (1953) (Kousser 1974; Issacharoff, Karlan, and Plides 1998). The partisan threat to the Democrats made them enable policies that continued their reign (Hudson 2011).

How were Democrats elected in the South to implement these policies? Republicans had worked to enfranchise African Americans after the Civil War. They also required voters to recite an oath of allegiance to the constitution to discourage still rebellious citizens from participating. This was seen as a violation and commitment to national union that irked many of the still loyal Southerners, as well as a threat to their way of life. As a result, many turned to the Democratic Party to continue their fight against northern interests. Democrats' regained power in most Southern states by the late 1870s in a period referred to as Redemption (NEH 2014; Davis n.d.). It was seen as a redemption of the Democratic Party by returning the South to "white rule" (Davis n.d.). The Redemption Movement was to force Northern Republicans back north and to reinstate white Southerners in places of power.

However, the Redemption Movement and the grandfather clause are not alone in the partisan activities that have contributed to a long history and developed into the current voting restrictions. The next section deals with one of the most daunting and influential of our partisan manipulations of voting laws—gerrymandering.

Gerrymandering/Redistricting

The literature on gerrymandering is vast. While this literature is divided on racial and partisan gerrymandering, we will focus on partisan gerrymandering in this chapter. Partisanship was a driving factor in redistricting postreconstruction and greatly affected African American voters (Clarke 2004). Literature climaxed in the 1980s and 1990s—with specific focus on partisan redistricting in the 1970s and 1980s (Neimi and Winsky 1992; Squire 1985; Cain 1985; Squire 1995). Research illustrates that there is a clear decrease in the number of house seats for the Democrats, while seeing an increase in proportion of the popular vote (Abramowitz 1983). Recent literature has focused on legislative composition at the state level (Shaffner et al. 2004), federal level (Albramowitz and Alexander 2006), voting behavior (Rush 2000; Desposato and Petrocik 2003; McKee 2008), polarization (Carson and Crespin 2007), and policy (Hayes, Hibbing, and Sulking 2010).

There are clear instances where partisanship influenced enforcement of voting rights protections, particularly when it came to preclearance provisions of Section 5 of the VRA (Epstein and O'Halloran 2006). Furthermore, this goes beyond the state legislature and affects the courts as well. McKenzie (2011) finds support for "constrained partisanship" in cases involving partisan gerrymandering, and where the law is clear judges will follow precedent on cases. However, when the law is ambiguous, there is a strong effect of party favoritism on judicial behavior in cases involving gerrymandering (McKenzie 2011) and as illustrated in *Rucho v. Common Cause* 2019.

The removal of Section 5 of the VRA opened the door to discrimination of all kinds (Cain 2013) including changes to redistricting plans. Moreover, scholars argue that racial and partisan gerrymandering are interconnected providing continued support to this book's overall argument about the three interconnected factors (Cox and Holden 2011; Epstein and O'Halloran 2006). Gerrymandering has clearly advantaged one party over another in state elections.

Often gerrymandering is presented as a Southern phenomenon but its historical roots are from outside of the region. Elbridge Gerry, the father of gerrymandering, was from Massachusetts, where he implemented the notorious redistricting plan in 1812. Furthermore, in 1888, Massachusetts was gerrymandered in favor of Jeffersonian Republicans, meaning that twenty-three out of twenty-six representatives were Republicans in safe seats (Upchurch 2004). At the time Kansas, Pennsylvania, and Illinois appeared to favor the GOP and Indiana, Ohio, Mississippi, and South Carolina favored the Democrats. Thus, redistricting is not just a one-party issue. Albeit it is often presented as a Republican tool, it certainly influences Democratic victories as well.

Felon Disenfranchisement

Felon disenfranchisement has often been connected to partisan policies. In this modern variation of a remaining Jim Crow-era law, Democrats have focused on the civil rights aspect of the law, while Republicans tend to focus on being tough on crime, leading both parties to oppose/support felon disenfranchisement accordingly (Conn 2004–5). As such, candidates and legislators are constrained by the ideological climate among a state's population (Burkhardt 2011).

The literature further demonstrates the partisan ties of the policy of felon disenfranchisement (Meredith and Morse 2015). Uggen and Manza (2002) and Manza and Uggen (2004, 2006) argue that Republican candidates benefit from felon disenfranchisement by removing typical Democratic voters from the voter pool, which guides the policies on continued disenfranchisement. While explaining opposition to a 2003 Alabama bill that would have made it easier for ex-felons to restore their voting rights, then Republican Party chairman Marty Connors is quoted as saying, "As frank as I can be, we're opposed to it because felons don't vote Republican" (as quoted in Meredith and Morse 2015), illustrating not only partisan policy preferences but also tangible partisan outcomes from continuing this policy. However, Hjalmarsson and Lopez (2010) and Burch (2012) argue the Republican bias is exaggerated as it helps/hinders both parties and both parties are responsible for redistricting maps that continue to lead to victories of their party. Burkhardt (2011) also suggests that policy liberalism appears to be more important than partisan strategizing for voter suppression in encouraging restoration of voting rights to felons and ex-felons.

Voter Identification

Voter identification laws are also plagued with partisan overtones. Some scholars have gone so far as to suggest that voter identification laws are a form of partisan engineering (Kellogg 2012). There has been an elevated discussion of electoral fraud and a resulting rhetoric around voter identification laws (Edelson et al. 2017). Voter identification is seen as a solution to the lack of confidence in the electoral system by ensuring that voters are properly identified prior to voting. Partisanship drives the discussion and cues for support of voter identification laws (Bowler and Donovan 2016;

Edelson et al. 2017). To provide some context to the value of voter identification laws to the outcome of elections, let us look at Wisconsin in 2016. For argument's sake, let us hypothesize that 10 percent of voters (mostly nonwhites and poor) are affected by voter identification laws. Wisconsin passed their voter identification law in 2011. Court filings revealed that 300,000 Wisconsin citizens lacked the type of identification required to vote (Smith 2019). In 2016, Donald Trump carried Wisconsin by 25,000 votes (a state that had not voted Republican for president for over thirty years) (Smith 2019). This shows the powerful effect on electoral outcomes by requiring voter identification.

Let us address some of the recent hyperbole around electoral fraud. Then candidate Trump argued that the "The System is Rigged" in a tweet leading up to the 2016 election and regularly suggested that if he didn't win that it was because of the election administration. This was not his sentiment alone—many voters have expressed concern about the security of our electoral process—be it nonregistered voters, Russian hacking, WikiLeaks, or more vaguely voter fraud. Revelations like those that emerged after the 2016 election about the activities of the Democratic National Committee during the Democratic primary have done little to alleviate these notions. At the same time that public skepticism about the reliability and veracity of elections entered the public dialogue, a series of election administration reforms has been taking place. The goals and outcomes of these reforms have been the subject of ongoing discussion and concern about their impact on voter access to the electoral process and a well-documented argument that we are more concerned with electoral security than accessibility. Legislators have capitalized on this threat and have often maintained their incumbency advantage by focusing on increasing the costs of voting especially for poor and minority voters.

Support for voter identification laws comes from partisan cues (Edelson et al. 2017; Atkeson et al. 2014; Alvarez et al. 2011). It is further conditioning support and belief in electoral activity. Democrats in states with strict photo identification laws are less confident in their states' elections but Republicans are more confident (Bowler and Donovan 2016). Further, discussion of electoral reform is also conditioned by partisan support with Democrats being more supportive and Republicans less supportive (Bowler and Donovan 2018; Atkeson et al. 2014). While there also is support from those who faced the barriers at the voting booth to reduce those barriers, partisanship appears to be the driving force behind current electoral standards—particularly when it comes to voter identification (Bowler and Donovan 2018). Bowler and Donovan find that there is evidence that despite years of working toward expanded voter opportunities, the recent shift is a result of two different causes: party and race (2018). First, the propensity to adopt more restrictive voting laws is greatest when control of the governor's office and the legislature switches to Republicans. Second, restrictions occur when the size of the black and Latino population in the state expands (Bowler and Donovan 2018).[3]

In general, Republicans and the states they have come to dominate have been the focus of these discussions and of the resulting concern of these practices. This focus is, at least in part, due to the empirical evidence that has demonstrated that increased voter access appears to benefit Democrats (see Hajnal, Lajevardi, and Nielson 2017; Highton 2017, Hicks, McKee, and Sellers 2015). As we noted in our earlier discussion of the partisan roots of election reform, it is clear that both parties have a history of using voting regulation and procedures to improve their odds of retaining political dominance and advantage.

These partisan motivations while clearly active in the decision-making process do not fully capture the motivation behind electoral reforms that increase voter obstacles. In fact, these partisan motivations often appear in concert with race-focused electoral reform. There exists a wealth of literature on how race plays a substantial and significant role in the electoral in the decision to make electoral changes. We explore these explanations and motivations in detail in the next chapter and we remain convinced that there exists a significant racial component that has emerged with the ascendency of the Alt Right in the Republican Party in year following the election of President Barack Obama in 2008, which became more prominent during the 2016 election. However, despite the ascendency of the Alt Right and the considerable attention paid to their influence in Republican politics, our own experience with studying voting behavior and observation of members of the Republican Party leaves us with the distinct feeling that something beyond simple partisanship or racism is likely going on.

Our experience and previous work on public policy issues lead us to ask whether these explanations are sufficient for explaining the totality of the Republican Party's policy positions regarding election administration and voter access. Among the most prevalent explanations for changes to voter access is partisan protectionism, and its accompanying attempts to increase the number of *your* party's voters that vote and decrease the number of the *other* parties. This notion has become so commonplace that it has developed into a game where voter motivation and turnout have displaced salient opinions and convincing arguments.

This horserace view of the electoral process has been well explored in the literature surrounding voter turnout, and where political parties focus their attention less on the swing voters whose minds may be changed and instead focus on motivating their own voters to turn out at higher rates than the other party. As this strategy has matured and become increasingly the most efficient approach available to the parties, they have turned their attention to institutional approaches that are likely to increase their voter's turnout in meaningful ways, or to limit the turn out of the other parties' voters.

In today's rhetoric, we see that the Republican Party has become known as the party of voter suppression, a bold statement that has historically (albeit alternatively) reflected the actions of both parties. Currently, there is seemingly a trend in Republican-held states to enact changes in voter law, which has been interpreted to mean policies of voter suppression. That sort of statement is an odd way to begin a discussion of what we believe to be an essential part of our understanding of how voting access changes came into vogue in the post-2008 era. While one cannot dismiss the role that both parties have played in changing voter laws to their advantage, this chapter will evaluate how the restrictions on voting access became a policy instrument of the Republican Party. Part of the potential motivation with voter suppression is due to there being more registered Democratic voters than any other party, so if all of these voters turned out and were spread across districts, elections may be solidly in the Democratic Party's pocket for decades.

Our intention with this book was never to evaluate the Republican Party, in fact, just the opposite. Our intent was to look at other factors outside of the party that contributed to the change in voting laws. However, the literature also indicates that this is something that needs, at a minimum, to be controlled for in this analysis. As noted in previous chapters, one cannot evaluate the threat behind voting restrictions without at least acknowledging partisan threat. In this institutional approach, the demographics of the two parties have led to two different approaches in making public policy. The common wisdom and much of the literature shows that as voting access is increased through longer voting hours, greater absentee voting, and generally through any institutional change, voting becomes easier. Due to the higher number of registered Democratic voters, additional turnout and access to voting would likely increase the vote share for Democratic Party. Thus, the expansion of voter access has a strong positive partisan effect for Democrats. The other side of this expansion is the view held by many Republicans, and generally confirmed by the literature, that new voters are more likely to vote Democratic. This limits the overall voter pool and creates strong partisan threats for Republicans. They are, therefore, much more likely to enact these institutional changes in an attempt to protect vote share, number of elected officials, dominance in legislatures, and policy influence.

In both cases, it should not be surprising that elected officials from both parties articulate support for the policy approach most likely to increase their voters even if it excludes others. This sort of partisan protectionism is designed to put into place institutional barriers to the other party enacting policy that can change the makeup of the electorate to favor their party's candidates, and as a result, their party's policy agenda is more likely to be enacted. This sort of naked partisanship has a long history in the United States and the focus of concern from the pre-constitutional era, by way of Federalist Paper 10. Madison wrote with great concern about the potential problems of faction in the new nation. Despite this concern, factions and eventually parties developed early, which has been one of the stickiest features of the US political system. These parties have sought their self-propagation through not just the battlefield that is American elections but also through institutional design that ensures their continued existence. This reality explains the relatively small number contemporary political parties, and the relatively small number of historical parties that have had significant influence over the last 200 plus years.

Despite the frequency of these attempts at partisan protectionism, there remains a general distaste for bald-faced partisanship in the United States and thus it is rare to see those engaging in public policy, especially those policies that are designed to change institutions, to favor one party over the other to acknowledge their goals explicitly. The reality, however, slips through occasionally and the recent race for Georgia governor is one such example.

The 2018 race for Georgia governor pitted the secretary of state, who is in charge of elections, a Republican, against a Democratic Georgia legislator. The race which had been polling as a close race saw the secretary of state and the Republican-dominated legislature engage in institutional changes, the chief of which was a requirement that names match the voter rolls exactly, a change that was fully expected to greatly advantage Republican candidates including the then secretary of state. The partisan reality was that because they could, Republicans in power engaged with the voting institutions in an attempt to influence the outcome. Other institutional tweaks were similarly used to advantage Republicans.

Thus, it is important to explore the role of partisanship in the 2018 election. No doubt, the Georgia governor's race received plenty of news coverage where partisanship and, arguably, race intersected to influence this election. The Georgia secretary of state, Brian Kemp, a candidate for governor, utilized the power of his office to determine which registrations would be rejected. This resulted in a constriction of ballots from Democratic (and black) voters, and while absolutely a power of the secretary of state, the critical factor was that those registrations that were rejected were overwhelmingly black and Democratic voters. Furthermore, on the day prior to the election, 3,000 voters were incorrectly flagged by the state as being ineligible, and another 53,000 voter registrations were delayed by Kemp's office without notification. Kemp refused to relinquish power over his office, despite the conflict of interest. Kemp meanwhile campaigned as being hard on immigration, nonpolitically correct leader that illustrated that the office of secretary of state has huge implications on the access to voting and whether a candidate should be able to hold that position during the election. These activities point to substantial political interference as well as racial overtones in the 2018 election administration. Seemingly, it is too challenging to leave election laws alone when they affect your political future. This case in Georgia, while primarily a partisan move, also had the ongoing subtext of race in the election as many of the excluded partisans were also minority voters. Like most of public policymaking, we find the voter access arena one where multiple motivations prevail and our attempts to understand it have led us to a strategy of attempting to tease the impact of each of the possible outcomes.

THREAT AND PARTISANSHIP

That elected officials act in their own self-interest, especially electorally, is neither new nor revolutionary. This reality has been well-demonstrated and the self-interested politician has become a near truism in most discussions of politics. Nevertheless, as with most decisions of the legislature and particularly with the distaste that most voters express at brazen partisan self-interest, something more is afoot. Our basic theory of what motivates the neo-populists policy preferences is the mitigation of threat, and even in the seemingly cut and dry world of partisan protectionism, we have seen this threat mechanism active. The ways in which partisan opponents and changes in partisan control are discussed and presented are clearly meant to engender a perception of threat that can be mitigated by voting for the "correct" political party.

We largely base our understanding of how partisanship would enter the legislative process and thereby become policy, as somewhat organic and as a natural outgrowth of the party's preferences simply becoming law. The reality is somewhat, although not dramatically, more complicated and substantial literature on how partisanship is active in the legislative decision-making process provides evidence that in the most polarized of issues (and there can be none more polarized than this one) partisanship is an active part of the decision-making process.

TESTING FOR THE EFFECTS OF PARTISANSHIP

As laid out in earlier chapters we believe that there are likely multiple motivations active in the decisions to adopt voter access restrictions, and that those motivations may all be present in any particular decision. Our own expectations certainly indicate that at least based on the anecdotal evidence, we have found there are few cases of single peaked motivation for these sorts of policy.

We again couch this expectation in our wider understanding of the threat literature, namely that partisans, and especially Republicans, are likely to respond to the changing demographics and the related partisan shifts with a threat response which creates an opening and provides the impetus for the adoption of policy measures that impact voter access. Here again, this threat is operative primarily because of the status quo bias, preferences of individuals and the likelihood of disruption, that shifts in demography are likely to mean.

In our exploration of this hypothesis we expect to find that any policy measure that increases voter access is likely to be negatively related to our measures of partisanship which include both legislative share held by Republicans, and the partisan affiliation of the governor and the chief elections officer—often the secretary of state.

Our expectation is that each of our partisan measures will be positively and significantly related our increased voter access restrictions across the states.

This chapter's focus is on the second set of hypotheses designed to test the well-documented connection between partisanship and voting restrictions addressed in the literature throughout this chapter.

Hypothesis 4: If there is Republican control of the legislature, then there will be an increase in voting restrictions.

Hypothesis 5: If there is Republican control of the executive branch, then there will be an increase in voting restrictions.

Hypothesis 6: If there is Republican control of multiple branches of government, then there will be an increase in voting restrictions.

Hypothesis 7: If there is a low margin of victory, then there will be an increase in voting restrictions.

Using partisanship as an explanation for voting restrictions means that states with more ideological split and/or states with large populations of the other party would be more likely to enact voting barriers as a way to continue and strengthen their party's stronghold in the state. Similarly, the margin of victory for one party over another may lead to a desire to increase that margin and provide more safe elections for the party. The desire for an increased margin of victory could result in voting suppression tactics of voters who are more likely to vote for the opposing party. Given the frame of Hypotheses 4, 5, and 6, we evaluate this as a function of Republican margin of victory in statewide races.

METHODS AND RESULTS

The analyses in this chapter are built around three partisan explanatory variables—partisan control of the legislature, partisan control of the governorship, and partisan control of the state's chief election officer (CEO). Along with these are interaction variables that account for the differing effects of control of separate combinations of Republican control of state institutions. Beyond these variables, these analyses also host the collection of control terms utilized in the previous chapter.

The partisan variables presented in this chapter are three different dichotomous partisan control terms. These terms accounted for distinctive partisan stances toward voting restrictions: Republican control over the state legislature, Republican control over the governorship, and Republican CEO. The legislative and gubernatorial terms are derived from summaries provided by the National Conference of State Legislatures (2019). The CEO variable is in most cases the secretary of state. While explanatory, some states lack a single such official and were dropped from the analysis. The result is the systematic exclusion of Delaware, Hawaii, New York, North Carolina, Oklahoma, and Pennsylvania in models that included the CEO. This exclusion is deemed not to significantly influence the conclusions of the analysis, so the term is included in all models that integrated partisanship. The CEO term is determined from data made available on individual state websites.

Included alongside these main partisan variables are all possible interactions between and among them. Specific combinations of partisan control for both the governorship and legislature under single-party control or control of both executive offices (governor and CEO) and the legislature are also included in this analysis. Holding multiple offices in government which influence voting policies would be theoretically more valuable than just one office in getting specific policies enacted. While having a higher-tier interaction introduced multicollinearity into the relevant models, this is an appropriate risk because of the theory-based necessity of the terms.

Table 5.1 Descriptive Statistics of Partisan Variables

	Minimum	Maximum	Mean	Std. Deviation	N
Republican Legislature	0	1	.434	.496	864
Republican Governor	0	1	.543	.499	864
Republican CEO	0	1	.564	.496	756
Republican Margin of Victory	−.569	.540	.041	.202	376

Source: Author.

Table 5.2 OLS Regression[4]: Registered Voters per Polling Place and Partisan Variables

	Model 1 +	Model 2
Rep Legislature	14.311 (169.598)	−31.689 (151.345)
Republican Gov	127.411 (130.075)	154.107 (111.001)
Republican CEO	−118.955 (169.598)	78.819 (149.333)
Rep Leg*Rep Gov	−461.077 (314.561)	−487.386 (266.711)
Rep Leg*Rep CEO	−230.259 (266.497)	−237.173 (231.230)
Rep Gov*Rep CEO	−245.957 (231.536)	−379.830 (198.311)
Rep Leg*Rep Gov*Rep CEO	815.518* (399.488)	760.254* (340.106)
GDP per Capita (thousands)		−.543 (4.732)
Spending per GDP		−99.548** (16.162)
Population (millions)		−6.596 (4.953)
Population Density (tens sq/mile)		5.068** (1.426)
West		108.703 (91.669)
South		64.217 (81.903)
Year		128.021** (19.578)
Constant	1647.779** (79.949)	2082.969** (340.956)
Obs	259	259
R2	.018	.297
F	1.657	8.804**

Source: Author.
**p value <.01; *p value<.05 +autocorrelation evident. Standard error in brackets.

Table 5.2 uses the election spending proxy as a dependent variable in this analysis of the dichotomous partisan control variables. While no lower-order terms were significant, total Republican control over the included offices of state government was seen to increase the number of registered voters per polling place in both models. This finding provides partial support for the expectations of Hypotheses 4 and 5 that Republican control of the legislature and governorship would lead to more restrictive voting policies—in this case a policy of lesser election spending leading to more crowded polling locations. However, these variables are only significant when in the presence of one another. Consistent with our previous findings, the significant and negative coefficient for spending percent of GDP provides some confidence into the accuracy of the chosen proxy, as it can be expected election spending would fall as relative economic resources contracted. However, none of the key independent partisan variables were significant.

Table 5.3 looks at the influence of partisan control on voting identification laws. In Model 1, Republican legislature and CEO separately are significant and when Republican legislature and governor are interacted we also see a significant and positive relationship. In Model 2, Republican legislatures and governors have no significant independent effects but together indicate 10.45 times higher odds of adopting more restrictive voter identification policies. The solitary presence of a Republican CEO, on the other hand, increased the

Table 5.3   Ordinal Regression: Voting ID Scale and Partisan Variables

	Model 1	Model 2
Rep Legislature	1.184** (.341)	.690 (.379)
Republican Gov	−.343 (.335)	−.171 (.359)
Republican CEO	1.299** (.295)	1.905** (.330)
Rep Leg*Rep Gov	3. 011** (.592)	3.233** (.629)
Rep Leg*Rep CEO	−.881 (.498)	−.070 (.534)
Rep Gov*Rep CEO	−.109 (.462)	−.735 (.499)
Rep Leg*Rep Gov*Rep CEO	−1.334 (.734)	−2.071** (778)
GDP per Capita (thousands)		−.023 (.012)
Spending per GDP		−.340** (.023)
Population (millions)		.008 (.014)
Population Density (tens sq/mile)		−.006 (.004)
West		−1.219** (.227)
South		.921** (.200)
Year		.248** (.023)
Obs	756	756
Chi-Square	270.919**	499.376**
Cox and Snell	.301	.483

Source: Author.
**p value <.01. Standard error in brackets.
Model 1: Goodness of Fit—Significant | Test of Parallel Lines—Significant.
Model 2: Goodness of Fit—Nonsignificant | Test of Parallel Lines—Significant.

odds of more restrictive policies by 3.63 times. What is interesting to note, however, is that the significant coefficient for total Republican control of government is negative. As a result, total Republican control of state governing institutions only makes more restrictive policies 9.41 times more likely—less than if Republicans only controlled the legislature and governorship. This suggests the possibly of diminishing returns from controlling additional offices but also appears to support the spirit of Hypothesis 6, which predicts that more Republican control of government would result in more restrictive voting identification laws.

Table 5.4 evaluates the partisanship independent variables regressed on the dependent variable of the scale of early voting policies. The expectations of Hypotheses 4 and 5 here would be to find negative coefficients on the partisan terms, indicating that Republican control made the enactment of less restrictive voting policies less likely. The anticipated results were realized for sole Republican control of the state legislature, which reduced the odds of less restrictive early voting policies in both models. Strangely, yet again greater control of the institutions of state government was not correlated with even lesser odds of unrestrictive voting policy. Republican control of only state legislature and governorship actually increased the odds of more expansive early voting policy by 1.08 times, and total Republican control of government

Table 5.4   Ordinal Regression: Early Voting Scale and Partisan Variables

	Model 1	Model 2
Rep Legislature	−1.316** (.324)	−1.495** (.343)
Republican Gov	−.482* (.233)	−.403 (.242)
Republican CEO	−.103 (.258)	−.070 (.277)
Rep Leg*Rep Gov	.985 (.543)	.735 (.557)
Rep Leg*Rep CEO	2.450** (.486)	2.533** (.502)
Rep Gov*Rep CEO	.362 (.378)	.509 (.392)
Rep Leg*Rep Gov*Rep CEO	−1.680** (.692)	−1.496** (.707)
GDP per Capita (thousands)		.022* (.011)
Spending per GDP		.110** (.037)
Population (millions)		.063** (.012)
Population Density (tens sq/mile)		.016** (.003)
West		−.420* (.191)
South		−1.567** (.190)
Year		−.011 (.018)
Obs	756	756
Chi-Square	48.802**	185.852**
Cox and Snell	.063	.218

Source: Author.
**p value <.01; *p value<.05. Standard error in brackets.
Model 1: Goodness of Fit—Significant | Test of Parallel Lines—Significant.
Model 2: Goodness of Fit—Nonsignificant | Test of Parallel Lines—Significant.

only yielded a cumulative odds ratio of 0.21 in the direction of more restrictive early voting policy. This provides mixed support for Hypotheses 4 and 5 but some support for the intuition of Hypothesis 6.

Table 5.5 tests the influence of partisan control on the enactment of online registration using a binary logistic regression. Model 1 has no significant results. However, the addition of the control variables in Model 2 results in a single significant partisan term—Republican control of state legislature. Online registration in this analysis is primarily explained by regional differences, relative expenditures, and diffusion over time. Online registration is an expansive activity so decreases in the odds of online registration as a function of a Republican legislature shows that there is still a decrease in voting access as noted in Hypothesis 4.

Table 5.6 provides an ordinal regression of the dependent variable permanent absentee policy and the independent partisan control variables. The main partisan variables are not significant in Model 1. Only one partisan variable was significant in Model 2—Republican control of the state legislature. The related coefficient was positive, however, suggesting that sole Republican control over the legislature also translates into greater odds of the existence of a permanent absentee list. It might help to make sense of this by noting that Republican control over only the legislature implicitly means Democratic control over the governorship and the position of CEO. Beyond this,

Table 5.5   Binary Logistic Regression: Online Registration and Partisan Variables

	Model 1	Model 2
Rep Legislature	−.376 (.430)	−1.213* (.604)
Republican Gov	−.381 (.323)	−.604 (.472)
Republican CEO	.259 (.321)	−.197 (.526)
Rep Leg*Rep Gov	.689 (.718)	.435 (.975)
Rep Leg*Rep CEO	−.175 (.640)	.541 (.913)
Rep Gov*Rep CEO	−.774 (.548)	−.389 (.786)
Rep Leg*Rep Gov*Rep CEO	.882 (.942)	.127 (1.303)
GDP per Capita (thousands)		−.017 (.017)
Spending per GDP		−.279** (.059)
Population (millions)		−.018 (.019)
Population Density (tens sq/mile)		−.002 (.006)
West		2.147** (.365)
South		.811* (.334)
Year		.543** (.048)
Obs	756	756
Constant	−1.155** (.181)	−3.976** (1.219)
Chi-Square	12.356	352.259**
Cox and Snell	.016	.372

Source: Author.
**p value <.01; *p value<.05. Standard error in brackets.

Table 5.6   Ordered Regression: Permanent Absentee and Partisan Variables

	Model 1	Model 2
Rep Legislature	.137 (.345)	.818** (.386)
Republican Gov	−.461 (.289)	−.469 (.314)
Republican CEO	.514 (.283)	.517 (.328)
Rep Leg*Rep Gov	−.262 (.667)	−.563 (.697)
Rep Leg*Rep CEO	−.129 (.511)	−.436 (.552)
Rep Gov*Rep CEO	−.349 (.449)	−.019 (.490)
Rep Leg*Rep Gov*Rep CEO	−.152 (.823)	−.393 (.864)
GDP per Capita (thousands)		−.041** (.014)
Spending per GDP		.146** (.045)
Population (millions)		.087** (.014)
Population Density (tens sq/mile)		.017** (.004)
West		1.373** (.234)
South		−1.103** (.259)
Year		.040 (.023)
Obs	756	756
Chi-Square	28.905**	174.314**
Cox and Snell	.038	.206

Source: Author.
**p value <.01. Standard Error in brackets.
Model 1: Goodness of Fit—Significant | Test of Parallel Lines—Significant.
Model 2: Goodness of Fit—Nonsignificant | Test of Parallel Lines—Significant.

Table 5.7   Binary Logistic: No-Excuse Absentee and Partisan Variables

	Model 1	Model 2
Rep Legislature	−.561 (.352)	−.585 (.406)
Republican Gov	−.162 (.258)	−.116 (.314)
Republican CEO	.103 (.286)	−1.034** (.416)
Rep Leg*Rep Gov	1.415* (.603)	1.261 (.677)
Rep Leg*Rep CEO	1.393** (.542)	1.894** (.666)
Rep Gov*Rep CEO	−.038 (.419)	1.093* (.556)
Rep Leg*Rep Gov*Rep CEO	−1.551* (.776)	−1.911* (.920)
GDP per Capita (thousands)		.004 (.016)
Spending per GDP		.093 (.052)
Population (millions)		.045* (.019)
Population Density (tens sq/mile)		−.012** (.004)
West		1.962** (.306)
South		−1.892** (.249)
Year		.034 (.025)
Obs	756	756
Constant	−.132 (.155)	−1.336 (1.060)
Chi-Square	28.394**	291.423**
Cox and Snell	.037	.320

Source: Author.
**p value <.01; *p value<.05. Standard Error in brackets.

the enactment of such policy is primarily explained by the control variables. Thus, it is possible that the effects of Democratic control of the executive offices in fact drive this policy enactment.

A final test of the restricted effects of partisan control is in the form of a binary regression utilizing the dependent variable of no-excuse absentee laws in table 5.7. In Model 1, the interaction terms of Republican legislature and Republican governor, as well as the interaction of Republican legislature and Republican CEO, are positive and significant. In Model 2, the main effects of legislature and governorship control are not significant, although the isolated presence of a Republican CEO is seen to reduce the odds of no-excuse absentee voting being implemented. Peculiarly, Republican control over just the legislature and governorship without the CEO actually indicates higher rather than lesser odds of the adoption of less restrictive policy. Full Republican control, on the other hand, just culminated into a potential cancellation of any partisan influence on the odds of adopting no-excuse absentee voting. This is in direct contracts to previous findings and is perhaps limited to no-excuse absentee laws.

We did countless analyses of the margin of victory to ascertain the motivation that a close election may have to a candidate and encourage them to implement laws to protect their seat in the next election. Regardless of the analysis—which variables were included or omitted—nothing was significant when it came to Hypothesis 7. Therefore, we must accept the null—that margin has no effect on voting access laws.

INTERACTION OF ECONOMIC AND PARTISAN INFLUENCES

After testing the restricted effects of partisanship on its own, the analysis moved on to investigating the combined effects of economics and partisan control. Included alongside the main economic and partisan terms were a number of interactions, which provided for the possibility that Republicans reacted differently to changes in revenues or expenditures. The results of those analyses are included here.

Table 5.8 provides a full model of partisan, economic, and control variables for each electoral law. The main economic terms were not significant in any of the models, and only one of the interactions between expenditure and partisan control was significant. Thus, for the most part, there was no evidence of the intuitions of the first three hypotheses. The significant interaction between expenditure and Republican control of the legislature in Model 2 was interesting. However, it seemed to suggest that an increased state budget partially mitigated the increased odds of more restrictive voting policy which actually supports Hypothesis 1 to some extent.

The primary partisan control terms were significant in table 5.8, Models 2, 3, 5, and 6. The expectation of Hypothesis 4 that Republican control of the legislature would result in more restrictive voting policy was met for voter identification laws (Model 2) and early voting (Model 3). It was reversed, however, for permanent absentee voting (Model 5) which saw increased odds of unrestrictive policy when there was a Republican legislature. Hypothesis 5 fared less well in table 5.8, with Republican control of the governorship having no significant effects. The presence of a Republican CEO, alternatively, did show an expected tendency toward more restrictive voting policy in the areas of voting identification (Model 2) and no-excuse absentee policies (Model 6). In the online registration model (Model 4), no significant effects of partisan control variables were found when the economic variables were added. This suggests that economic concerns may mitigate partisanship in these areas.

The interaction effects between partisan control variables complicate the results further. Republican control of a state's governorship and CEO correlates with a decline in number of voters per polling place, for instance, both reversing the expectations of more restrictive voting conditions in that case, as well as severely reducing the effect of total Republican control which had the anticipated coefficient direction. This theme of decreasing or totally

Table 5.8 Economic and Partisan Models

	Model 1 Registered Voters per Polling Place	Model 2 Voter ID	Model 3 Early Voting	Model 4 Online Reg	Model 5 Perm Absentee	Model 6 No-Excuse absentee
Rep Legislature	-116.501 (168.417)	1.039* (.418)	-1.757** (.389)	-1.278 (.671)	.911* (.440)	-.899 (.473)
Republican Gov	18.425 (136.159)	-.179 (.417)	-.377 (.308)	-.103 (.528)	-.598 (.390)	.354 (.414)
Republican CEO	245.459 (196.953)	1.841** (.428)	.333 (.369)	-.447 (.675)	.782 (.432)	-1.247* (.530)
Rep Leg*Rep Gov	-366.625 (272.439)	3.435** (.651)	.739 (.582)	.367 (1.007)	-.402 (.719)	1.144 (.699)
Rep Leg*Rep CEO	-282.200 (239.496)	-.107 (.553)	2.527** (.528)	.514 (.953)	-.482 (.580)	1.985** (.699)
Rep Gov*Rep CEO	-451.437* (207.853)	-.807 (.517)	.344 (.409)	-.193 (.818)	.036 (.510)	1.178* (.585)
Rep Leg*Rep Gov*Rep CEO	684.246* (344.296)	-2.059** (.802)	-1.366 (.734)	.162 (1.334)	-.614 (.893)	-1.883* (.952)
GDP per Capita (thousands)	-1.948 (4.953)	-.019 (.013)	.022 (.012)	-.020 (.018)	-.035* (.015)	.003 (.017)
Spending per GDP	-106.382** (16.712)	-.330** (.049)	.106** (.038)	-.282** (.061)	.155** (.047)	.081 (.055)
Population (millions)	-6.625 (5.085)	.005 (.015)	.066** (.012)	-.019 (.020)	.086** (.015)	.047* ((.020)
Population Density (tens sq/mile)	5.030** (1.471)	-.004 (.004)	-.017** (.003)	-.001 (.006)	.017** (.004)	-.012** (.004)
West	124.406 (92.071)	-1.167** (.234)	-.516** (.200)	2.171** (.372)	1.465** (.249)	2.055** (.334)
South	63.156 (83.204)	-.864** (.207)	-1.682** (.200)	.777* (.337)	-1.094** (.269)	-1.913** (.259)

	Model 1	Model 2	Model 3	Model 4	Model 5	Model 6
Year	132.378**	.225**	−.005	.559**	.036	.042
	(20.527)	(.025)	(.020)	(.050)	(.025)	(.028)
Revenue Percent Change	4.286	−.010	−.004	.018	.011 (	.029
	(15.527)	(.028)	(.026)	(.056)	(.037)	(.046)
Expenditure Percent Change	−3.822	−.052	.000	.065	−.040	.031
	(19.254)	(.030)	(.028)	(.060)	(.038)	(.051)
Revenue*Rep Leg	−6.528	.058	−.026	.083	−.019	−.032
	(19.820)	(0.45)	(.041)	(.071)	(.050)	(.058)
Revenue*Rep Gov	8.997	−.017	.017	−.045	.062	.036
	(17.799)	(.045)	(.037)	(.070)	(.047)	(.055)
Revenue*Rep CEO	−13.250	.004	−.015	−.056	−.043	−.010
	(21.927)	(.052)	(.044)	(.079)	(.053)	(.062)
Expend*Rep Leg	21.419	−.110*	.040	−.010	.009	.095
	(20.554)	(.049)	(.044)	(.080)	(.056)	(.062)
Expend*Rep Gov	26.263	.007	−.019	−.127	−.009	−.111
	(20.211)	(.051)	(.043)	(.077)	(.052)	(.061)
Expend*Rep CEO	−23.163	.033	−.045	.053	.029	.015
	(22.363)	(.053)	(.046)	(.084)	(.058)	(.063)
Obs	259	714	714	714	714	714
Constant	2221.456**			−4.275*		
	(368.152)			(1.276)		
Chi-Square		485.528**	193.543**	337.461**	174.645**	285.172**
R2	.295					
Cox and Snell		.493	.237	.377	.127	.329

Source: Author.

**p value <.01; *p value<.05. Standard Error in brackets.

Model 1 is an OLS regression; Models 2, 3, and 5 are ordinal regressions; Models 4 and 6 are Binary Logistic Regressions.

reversing results when additional partisan control is present in four of the six regressions.

CONCLUSION

Our findings from this chapter show mixed results for partisanship affecting the enactment of voting restriction policies. Partisanship appears to be significant for voter identification laws and to some extent early voting. Nevertheless, the inclusion of economic variables often mitigates or reverses these findings.

Despite this reality, however, as our examination of the modern Republican Party indicates, articulating these policies in terms of the fiscal threat costs that expanded voter access may have is likely to mollify some parts of the Republican coalition that are necessary to policy adoption on a widespread scale. Thus, indicative of support for the theory of Fiscal Conservatives as the "Baptists" in the fundamental theory of Baptists and Bootleggers provides cover for more nefarious motivations. We explore additional motivations in the next chapter examining minority populations as a causal factor in enactment of these laws.

NOTES

1. In this case, the court ruled that partisan gerrymandering in North Carolina presents political questions beyond the reach of the federal court system.

2. Clearly there were discriminatory laws prior to the Civil War when it came to voting rights—voting was typically reserved for free white, Protestant, property-owning men over the age of twenty-one.

3. This second part will be addressed with Hypotheses 8a and 8b in the race chapter.

4. We understand there is multicollinearity with including the interaction terms; however, their significance and theoretical support illustrate that they should be included.

Chapter 6

Racial Influences

The rhetoric surrounding the 2016 and 2018 elections clearly illustrates the role that race has continued to play in American politics. Certainly, many scholars hoped that we were post-racial with the election of President Obama in 2008. However, the continued racial divide in our country indicates otherwise. Historical evidence to follow illustrates that race has played a large role in the development of voting barriers.

The recent passage of new restrictions (even under the VRA) that continue to disenfranchise and make voting more difficult have been formulated, adopted, and implemented across the United States. These restrictions are both covert and overt, much like their earlier predecessors. That said, based on our understanding of the policy formulation and adoption process particularly in this area, we propose that it is not simply a case of racial or ethnic animus driving the policy process, although it is clearly present in the policy discussion.

Race lacks the mechanism for policymaking. Further, we believe that race alone is too easy an explanation—instead we propose that like most policy formulations it is a complex discussion, where race plays an integral but not solitary role in the adoption of restrictions to voting access. As such, our commitment to exploring economic and partisanship explanations in tandem with race is evident throughout this book.

We begin our discussion of this complex policy process with an exploration of the important role that race has had on the policy process. In this chapter, we explore the racial overtones from the 2008 election and beyond as well as the historical inlays of race and voting restrictions. We then look at the impact race has held on the development of these new restrictions, and provide empirical evidence for the influence of race in the adoption of some of the new voting rights restrictions.

During the 2008 election, race was without question a major factor in voting (on both sides) as well as a defining part of the rhetoric and electoral campaign. The 2008 election sparked discussions about race in America that had laid dormant since the discussion of welfare queens and the subtle racism that had been present in the 1988 campaign. These discussions were in part driven by the selection of an African American nominee by the Democrats. The focus on this admittedly historic selection made race a topic at the forefront of the campaign. While this selection brought the issue front and center, long-simmering racial issues and prejudice remained and there is strong evidence that racial prejudice contributed to vote choice in 2008 and subsequent elections (Piston 2010). Racial stereotypes of Blacks have an impact on the vote choice of white voters. This impact was also manifested among independent white voters, and Republican white voters (who were already unlikely to vote for a Democrat) who were even less likely to vote for Obama than for previous Democratic candidates because of his race (Piston 2010; Mas and Moretti 2009). Voters, especially independents, were more likely to vote third party or abstain rather than cast a ballot for Obama (Payne et al. 2010). There is a wealth of evidence that demonstrates that the bulk of the support necessary for candidates to win comes from the loyalists of one's own party, and thus it appears that the overall outcome of the election may have been little impacted by the racial prejudice (Mas and Moretti 2009).

DID 2008 MATTER?

On the surface, the 2008 election was monumental. Not only was a member of a racial minority selected as a majority party candidate, he won the presidency. Thus, a member of a race, for whom the VRA was written to protect, occupied the White House (Ansolabehere, Persily, and Stewart 2009). While the election was monumental in so many ways, it sparked many new areas of debate, such as the relevance of the VRA, a new voting bloc, and even more racially polarized elections (Ansolabehere, Persily, and Stewart 2009).

Purely from an electoral turnout perspective, there were higher numbers of black voters who participated in the election, and Obama did better among minority voters than previous candidates. However, electorally in the Deep South, Obama did worse than John Kerry had among white voters. In swing states, Obama did better among white voters than John Kerry had four years earlier. In states not covered by the VRA, Obama did not do as well among white voters (Ansolabehere, Persily, and Stewart 2009). These realities illustrate the complex nature of the impact of race on elections and point to a more nuanced discussion where race is an important factor but not the solitary one.

Further illustrating this complexity, many of new voting blocs did not show up to reelect Obama in 2012, indicating that there had not been a fundamental shift in voter turnout and participation across the United States.

OBAMA EFFECT AND THE 2008 CAMPAIGN

The complexities that the 2008 campaign points to can be further illustrated by some of the discussions of race that arose during the course of the campaign. These discussions unlike what so many would have predicted were not simply a question of the cross-racial concern and prejudice. Obama's race, having been born to a white mother and African father and its seeming relevance to the campaign, led some to raise questions of who did Obama represent, even if just symbolically? African Americans wondered whether Obama was "Black enough" while whites wanted reassurances that Obama was not "too Black" (Sinclair-Chapman and Price 2008). This added level of complexity and the odd quandary it placed in racial discussions and associations is illustrative of our understanding of the complex role that race places in the electoral process. That race was active is demonstrated by the number of well-respected white endorsers who enabled Obama to be seen as a "different kind of Black candidate" and protect him from charges that he was part of the radical black left (Sinclair-Chapman and Price 2008).

The antiblack sentiment that had been part of the Southern strategy in the 1980s continued to be part of the conversation, at least covertly (Sinclair-Chapman and Price 2008). The implicit racial cues (Mendelberg 2001) were countered by the Obama campaign frequently, and limited the use of them on the federal level. Further, then candidate McCain refused to engage the racial issues in his campaign rhetoric, although his supporters were somewhat less restrained. The 2008 campaign, at least by the two presidential candidates, focused on policy and personality. However, the racial difference was "an inescapably noticeable feature of the election" (Greenwald et al. 2009). Undoubtedly, race played a role in the vote choice and electability of the candidates.

THE OBAMA YEARS

This complexity increased during the Obama years as racial images, conversations, and speeches continued in abundance. President Obama himself addressed race in a number of his speeches (Wingfield and Feagin 2012) and there was some relatively high-minded discussion about the potential for a post-racial society that could be emerging. The reality, however, was somewhat less high-minded and the coverage of the Obama family and discussions surrounding the president and his presidency sharply illustrate the remaining prejudice in American politics and society. Beginning with the now legendary discussion over his birth certificate, to how he was portrayed in satire race came to permeate some of the criticisms of the president and his administration.

There was an increase through both Obama terms "in openly and blatantly racist rhetoric, language, and imagery that has regularly mocked President Obama, his wife and daughters, and Black Americans more broadly" (Wingfield and Feagin 2012). There were a number of cartoons depicting the president as a monkey, online discussions describing Obama's children as "ghetto hoochies," and a sharp rise in hate group membership (Wingfield and Feagin 2012). These issues became so pervasive that the NAACP issued statements against these depictions and statements, taking to task the outlets that covered them and therefore gave them wider reach (Wingfield and Feagin 2012).

Candidates who ran for any number of elected offices during this time ran against Obama, and, at times, were openly racist (Wingfield and Feagin 2012). It is rare in the post-civil rights era to find the use of implicit racial messages in Democratic primaries as was seen in the 2008 election cycle (Sinclair-Chapman and Price 2008). Despite increase in racialized campaign rhetoric, this period was also a substantial victory for minority rights as the nomination and eventual election of a minority candidate on a major party ticket had profound implications.

POST-RACIAL?

Immediately after the 2008 election, many argued that 2008 marked a major change in race relations, and even ushered in a "post-racial" era (Mukherjee 2016). If we have learned anything since 2008, this is far from the case. The rhetoric surrounding the 2016 election and the continued racial issues that confront the country demonstrate that race is forefront in people's minds and continues to be a major factor in American politics and society. Many commentators argued that Obama's election created a "post-racial" period, where race would be a less significant determinant of outcomes, opportunities, and chances (Wingfield and Feagin 2012). However, the depiction of Obama throughout his presidency and the realities of electoral campaigns during the Obama administration illustrate that celebrations and high-minded commentary of post-racial America were premature and fundamentally flawed (Wingfield and Feagin 2012).

While many can argue that they are not prejudiced, and despite the increasing social pressure to not express racists attitudes, there remains significant negative perceptions of out-groups (Augoustinos and Every 2007). In short, racial attitudes continue and have in some cases been inflamed (Bloch 2014). Those who felt the repercussions of the economic downturn of 2008 and the following years lashed out against Obama, blacks, and nonwhite immigrants (Bonilla-Silva 2013; Brettell and Nibbs 2011; Douglas, Sáenz, and Murga 2015). These attitudes drove much of the rhetoric of the 2016 election.

Some of the most interesting evidence cutting against the post-racial hypothesis is from Bonilla-Silva and Forman (2000) who find that white respondents are more likely to use economic terms to hide their racial attitudes and when those terms are considered, appear more prejudiced that before. They further find that surveys have underestimated the extent of prejudice that still exists in the white population and that the legal and normative changes in the United States post-1960s have created a new racial perspective: color-blind racism (Bonilla-Silva and Forman 2000).

"Color-blind" racism is a term used when racial issues become part of the climate of the country that allows for ambivalence, apparent non-racialism, and slipperiness on racial issues (Bonilla-Silva 2002). Bonilla-Silva (2002) discusses five components of this theory: (1) whites' dodging direct racial language, (2) the central rhetorical strategies used by all whites to safely express their racial views, (3) the role of projection, (4) the role of diminutives, and (5) how intrusions into forbidden issues produce incoherence among many whites.

Taken together the high-minded claims of a post-racial America fall apart rather quickly and the political climate since 2008 that led to the development of the Alt Right is neither unexpected nor surprising. Hawley talks about the responses to the notion of the "post-racial" America and the development of a vulgar, racist movement (2017). Hawley acknowledges the role that Barack Obama and Hillary Clinton had in creating this backlash while looking at how the Alt Right also differs from traditional conservatism. The development of the Alt Right and how what had been relegated to the extreme fringes of a major political party has come to have substantial influence on public policy discussion where race is clearly an active factor of particular interest to those that study public policy and electoral process. Too little substantive discussion of the circumstance and situation has allowed this to occur. Instead, the blinding racism of the Alt Right has dominated discussions and as a result left the mechanism of this ascendency too little understood.

PERCEIVED THREAT TO WHITES

One of the underlying issues in American politics has been racial threat. One only needs to look at the success of Donald Trump to see how that threat theory can be readily mobilized, weaponized, and ultimately used to win elections and change public policy. That said, a full discussion of racial threat theory is necessary and provided in the theory chapter, to understand how race has played a role in the changes to voting mechanisms post-2008.

The US population has become more racially and ethnically diverse. By 2050, the expectation is that the nonwhite population will eclipse the white population in size (Colby and Ortman 2014). This changing landscape of the American population creates a different dynamic and for some, a sense of threat to their place in society. The perception of these threats leads to many decisions (voting, policy, and even rhetoric) that continue to divide our country based on race. To that end, the United States' party system will shift because of this racial diversity. Chris Jankowski, a Republican strategist, suggested, "if we [Republicans] continue to underperform in this multiracial world that is going to be America, and the white voters are going to be a clear minority, the Republican Party will cease to exist" (Smith 2019). This illustrates just how much this changing demography creates partisan and racial threats.

RACIAL THREAT THEORY

As we have laid out in chapter 2, much of our understanding of the racial motivation for public policy, especially electoral access policy, is rooted in threat theory, and in its particular application as racial threat theory. Racial threat theory argues that majority race (white) members' feel threatened about their place in society when other racial groups emerge, assert some power, or change the social dynamics of society. These have been well cataloged in midcentury literature (Allport 1954; Ashmore and DelBoca 1976; LeVine and Campbell 1972). There are related theories that also illustrate white prejudice: realistic group conflict theory (examines the tangible threat blacks pose to whites) and a sociocultural theory of prejudice (subjects are socialized into moralistic resentments of blacks) (Kinder and Sears 1981). With threat perception activated, public policy actions that seek to return to the previous status quo and advantaged position become attractive in an attempt to mitigate the perceived threat. Thus, in periods where the majority group is under pressure, threat activation can be used to pursue policies that absent the perceived threat would be unpalatable, and when coupled with other arguments for their implementation can lead to policies advocated by those with substantial racial animus (like the Alt Right). Despite claims that there has been a decrease in the perception of racial threat, a raft of explorations and solid evidence from recent electoral cycles lend strong support to its importance and role in policymaking (Tolbert and Grummel 2003; Stephan, Ybarra, and Bachman 1999).

Immigrant Threat (and Connected Racial Threat)

While traditional racial threat theory is clearly active in the discussions of electoral discussion, changing demographics and circumstance have led many to posit an application of the theory beyond the traditional black/white racial threat literature. This expansion has focused on immigration and the perceived threat of immigrant populations to the status quo. In electoral discussions, the role of immigration and the impact of immigrant populations are paramount.

In this case, race and especially nonnative status permeate the political discourse. Teasley and Ikard (2010) examine prejudice toward immigrants through four theories (realistic threats, symbolic threats, intergroup anxiety, and negative stereotyping). They find support for all four theories in predicting attitudes toward immigrants (this is particularly important given that their experimental group involve students who tend to be more liberal on immigration attitudes) (Teasley and Ikard 2010).

This intolerance toward immigrants is not new, and American history is replete with anti-immigrant bias (Fuchs 1995; Takaki 1989). An important caveat is that the country of origin for the immigrant has often greatly impacted this process, where groups perceived to be more similar to the existing dominant group are viewed with less hostility, and further reinforces the threat hypothesis. Teasley and Ikard suggest that there has been a recent increase in hostility toward immigrants (2010). Abrajano and Hajnal (2015) in their book *White Backlash* show that fears about immigration fundamentally influence white Americans' core political identities, policy preferences, and electoral choices. They further argue that these fears and the changing policy approaches of the major parties led to a large-scale defection of whites from the Democratic to the Republican Party. They point out that what they term "blacklash" has important implications for the future of race relations in the United States (Abrajano and Hajnal 2015).

They argue, and we largely agree, that growing racial and ethnic diversity in the United States has transferred to a greater racial divide in politics—the right-left continuum demonstrates that whites are moving more right and minorities more to the left. The implications of this for future political discussions and policy formulation are that greater focus on race and the role of pressure from changing demographics are likely to dominate many policy discussions, including those around voting access and electoral rules. Beyond this, Abrajano and Hajnal (2015) suggest that these racial divisions will outweigh class, age, gender, and other demographic measures.

In the discussion of voting restrictions one group of recent immigrants largely dominates, namely Latinos. The role of Latinos in the discussion of voting restrictions goes without saying. The growth of Latino immigration and population growth (and accompanying media coverage) powered the white backlash to protect issues of voting and border security (Abranjano and Hajnal 2015). Here again, it is relatively clear most of the policy propositions are designed to mitigate perceived threat. A short review of the claims made regarding immigration quickly reveals attempts to mitigate the economic, social or political impact of this group on the status quo.

These threats have also served partisan purposes, in that the backlash was against the Democratic party and supportive of the Republican Party (and reflective of their bases—younger, minority, poorer vs. older, whiter, wealthier). Thus, racial explanations and partisan explanations can appear to be linked (Stephan, Ybarra, and Bachman 1999; Abranjano and Hajnal 2015).

TRUMP . . .

The election of Donald Trump can be seen as a backlash to the presidency of Barack Obama. The Trump administration, and the president himself, is the antithesis of the Obama administration in nearly every way—policy, demeanor, experience, race, talking points, and statesmanship (McGettigan 2016). While Obama represented hope and change to many voters in America, he also was what many most feared (McGettigan 2016). The changing demographics of the United States and the expectation that nonwhites will outnumber whites by 2042 contributed to the success of Donald Trump in 2016. Building off the racial threat theories discussed earlier, the electoral success of Trump is clearly rooted in the causal mechanisms advanced by threat theory (Major, Blodorn, and Blascovich 2016).

The Trump campaign quickly racialized immigrant groups and claims about their threat to American values, prosperity, and the social order quickly became a central, yet controversial, aspect of his campaign. This focus led many to make accusations of racism (Subtirelu 2017). Online communities of Trump supporters adamantly denied that Trump's statements or policy proposals were racist—drawing many to make the parallel to color-blind racism (Subtirelu 2017). Indeed, this parallel appears particularly cogent given the threat-based rhetoric that the campaign actively used. In contrast, Trump campaign supported and argued that making connections to racism were political tactics and should be disregarded (Subtirelu 2017). Regardless of the motivation, these policies and statements had broad emotional appeal to many voters, an appeal we believe is rooted in threat theory and a desire to mitigate the threat by eliminating immigration and returning to a perceived previous status quo. It is in the context of a complex racial political reality that our discussion of the mechanisms of voter access restriction begins.

RACIAL COMPONENTS TO ELECTION BARRIERS

Literacy tests did not originate in the South but out of the same belief of preventing voting among undesirable voters. Early examples in Massachusetts (1857)—Article XX established a literacy test and added this provision: "this amendment shall not apply to any person . . . who now has the right to vote, nor any person who shall be sixty years of age or upward at the time this amendment shall take effect." The partisan history of the Massachusetts' bill is that it originated with the American Party (also known as the Know Nothing Party). Later in 1858, the legislature, as well as the governor and lieutenant governor, moved to a Republican majority. The American Party was openly anti-Catholic, xenophobic, and hostile to immigration, which was the foundation of this early literacy test. The literacy test then proliferated in the South based on the constitutionality of the Massachusetts's precedent. Since the literacy test was acceptable in Massachusetts and was not seen as a vehicle blocking black voters, Southern states argued that the same principles that applied in Massachusetts about wanting qualified voters could be extended to other states (NPR 2013).

Proponents of the literacy test suggested that a voter required the ability to read and understand English. They claimed that the exams ensured that voters were well-informed and educated prior to voting. However, in practice it was different. They were used to disqualify ethnic voters in the South—namely African American voters. In the North, they were used to disqualify immigrants and the poor. In some states, the literacy test rose to a new level. In Mississippi, for example, those registering to vote were required to transcribe and interpret a section of the state constitution and write an essay on the responsibilities of citizenship. The official that was registering voters selected the question and decided which answers were passing/failing. Thus, the election official had the ability to determine which potential registrants would be successful.

Literacy Tests and Property Qualifications

Lawmakers in Mississippi had to choose between property and literacy requirements. They chose literacy. Literacy was the "only solution to the race problem that would command the approval of a majority of people of the North" (Upchurch 2004: 113). John Tyler Morgan in defense of the voting restrictions suggested that "we, the people" was not intended to include blacks but rather only white voters (Upchurch 2004: 114). Morgan and his fellow Southern Democrats were concerned about the different standards that Northern states were subjected to as compared to Southern states arguing that the Fifteenth Amendment needed to be applied equally (Upchurch 2004), which is also the premise of the *Shelby County* case. He argued that Massachusetts enacted a literacy test in 1857 for the sole purpose of controlling the voting strength of their ethnic immigrant populations (Upchurch 2004). How was that not a violation while the Southern literacy tests were? Southern Democrats fought hard for their new voter qualifications, believing that Republicans had placed prohibitions on these types of qualifications during Reconstruction as Confederate states were readmitted to the Union (Upchurch 2004: 115). George Frisbie Hoar, one of the architects of Reconstruction, was ultimately the lynchpin in Mississippi adopting literacy tests (and their spread across the South). Hoar was asked during the debate on the Blair Education Bill if literacy tests could be adopted in Mississippi as they had been in Massachusetts. He said yes as long as they were applied equally to both races (Upchurch 2004). While comical in its naiveté particularly at this time, this set the standard for voting restrictions across the South.

The failure of the Federal Elections Bill in 1890 after Democratic filibusters and obstructionism led the development of widespread Jim Crow laws (Upchurch 2004). There were a number of cases that challenged the Jim Crow laws—*Mills v. Green* (1895); *Giles v. Harris* (1903); *Guinn v. United States* (1915) among them, but the laws continued to proliferate and continue to discriminate against voters (Riser 2010). It was a generally accepted practice to block black voters (*Sproule v. Fredericks* 1892) (Riser 2010). Some of these practices included requiring voters to register the year they were first eligible or not be allowed to vote—*Mills v. Green* (1895), the grandfather clause, literacy tests, and poll taxes.

Felon Disenfranchisement

As explored earlier, felon disenfranchisement laws do have partisan overtones—but they also have racial overtones. These laws continue to affect (disproportionally) racial minorities and low-income voters, due to longstanding and well-documented racial gaps in poverty and incarceration rates. Florida restored voting rights to felons through a ballot measure in 2019, followed by legislation with the caveat that convicted felons must pay all court-ordered financial obligations (including court fees) prior to voting, which is rhetorically being compared to a poll tax (Madani 2019). However, the average annual income is $6,500 for those newly out of prison (Madani 2019). To further demonstrate how the felon disenfranchisement disproportionally affected minority voters, 20 percent of Florida's black adults were prevented from voting under the felon disenfranchisement law. This signals that the felon disenfranchisement laws have not only partisan but also racial implications.

Unquestionably, we believe that race has played a substantial role in the development of voting restrictions. Historical understandings of the VRA illustrate how minority voters have been systematically prevented from voting, and the motivations of most of these restrictions are clear. Our review of the history strongly suggests that these motivations were closely tied to and were the primary motivation for these restrictions. What also became clear in our reading of the historical treatment of these restrictions was that these restrictions were always coupled with something more than just simple racial animosity (although it was most often present), that then provided the mechanism for the adoption of the restrictions across the United States. This understanding was true from early immigrant voting restrictions in the Northeast, to the more commonly discussed Jim Crow restrictions. The pairing of racial or ethnic animus with partisanship and other policy issues is readily apparent.

As noted earlier, redistricting has partisan as well as racial aspects. Race-based redistricting has two general variations—packing and cracking. Packing is when we create minority-majority districts to assist minority populations in creating better representation but also prevents minority voters from having influence in several districts. However, scholars have found that minority-majority districts lead to less support from members elected with smaller minority populations (Overby and Cosgrove 1996). Cracking is when like-minded voters or voters of a particular racial group are spread across several districts to dilute the power of their vote (Shepherd 1994; *Shaw v. Reno* 1994; Niemi et al. 1990). There is a great deal of evidence to suggest that this leads to black voter vote dilution (Wolf 1997; Waymer and Heath 2016).

Race-based redistricting resulted in a realignment of Southern legislatures (Lublin and Voss 2000) and affected legislation because of the type of representatives elected (Sharpe and Garand 2001). Racial redistricting harmed Democrats' ability to win control of state houses (Lublin and Voss 2000). Racial gerrymandering (as it refers to cracking) has been struck down by the court (*Shaw vs. Reno* 1993) but minority-majority districts can be drawn that concentrate black (and Democratic) voters in one district creating more Republican districts throughout the state (Epstein and O'Halloran 2006). When redistricting is done in this manner, it is clear that gerrymandering has both racial and partisan effects.

Race and Voter Identification Laws

As we have previously illustrated, a plethora of voting barriers have historically limited minority voters, for example, grandfather clauses, Jim Crow laws, poll taxes, and whites-only primaries. Unlike these traditional forms of voter suppression that the VRA and other policy reforms in middle part of the twentieth century sought to eliminate, new forms of voting obstacles have emerged. These obstacles have primarily taken the form of voter identification laws, and decreased hours for registration and voting. Voter identification laws require that voters provide government-issued (or endorsed) identification prior to casting their ballots on Election Day. These types of laws were designed at the behest of officials who argued that they were needed to prevent voter fraud, and the perceived threat that fraud represented. These laws are relatively new—most passed post-2008. These laws then affect groups with lower levels of political awareness, low-income and racial minorities more than other groups (Hajnal, Lajevadri, and Nielson 2017). There is also clear evidence that voter identification laws skew electoral results toward those on the political right (Hajnal, Lajevadri, and Nielson 2017).

Public opinion on these laws is often driven by personal experience, anecdote, and media coverage. There appears to be a gap in opinion between liberals and conservatives (Wilson and Brewer 2013). The discussion of these restrictions, particularly from their proponents, is generally focused on claims that voter fraud represents a substantial threat to the policymaking process and Democratic institutions. These perceptions are closely linked to the beliefs about the prevalence of actual voter fraud and the risk it poses.

EFFECT OF LAWS ON RACIAL MINORITIES

While the impetus for the change in laws may be still up for discussion, the effect of the laws on particular voting blocs is not. First, they are not uniformly applied. Laws involving voter identification are more likely to be applied if the voter is a member of a racial minority. Research from New Mexico showed that Latino, male, and Election Day voters were more likely to be required to show identification than non-Latino, female, and early voters (Atkeson et al. 2010). This held regardless of the partisanship or ethnicity of the poll workers implementing the requirement (Atkeson et al. 2010). Furthermore, these laws also discourage voter turnout, particularly among minority voters, who are somewhat less likely to have the required documentation readily available (Sobel and Smith 2009).

There have been notable arguments about the role of these voter identification laws. The Brenna Center for Justice argues that voter identification laws serve as barriers to participation among legitimate racial and ethnic minority voters as well as others from disadvantaged groups (Weiser 2014). Eric Holder, former US attorney general, equated voter identification laws to a poll tax placed on particular voters (Hajnal, Lajevardi, and Nielson 2017). Justice Ruth Bader Ginsburg has called voter identification laws as "purposely discriminatory" for racial minorities (Lowry 2014). Finally, the Voting Rights Institute argues that these laws are "an unnecessary, expensive, and intrusive voter restriction" (Voting Rights Institute 2015). For some, the growth of voter identification laws and the suppression of voters represents a substantial civil rights issue. However, critics of voter identification laws also find few instances of voter fraud and thus little reason to enact these laws (Hajnal, Lajevardi, and Nielson 2017).

Given the relative proximity of the implementation of these barriers to voting access, an examination of the motivations becomes relatively clear. As a result, we have proposed a three-pronged theory demonstrating that it is the interplay between race, partisanship, and economics that drives these decisions. We thus begin our discussion of this interplay with an examination of the role that race plays in the adoption of voting rights restrictions.

This chapter allows us to explore hypotheses relating to state racial compositions and their connection to the implementation of voting restrictions, as well as the interaction of all three factors together. We evaluate black and Latino populations separately in these analyses. We did evaluate the minority population as a whole in separate analyses but found that it was neither descriptive nor theoretically relevant. Additionally, the significance of the compounded variable was not any different than the separate variable analysis.

RESULTS

The final set of explanatory independent variables we analyze are the race variables, included to assess the impact of minority populations on the political calculations behind voting restrictions. Black and Latino percentage of the population are chosen from among all statistics for their significant presence in many state elections. This is also consistent with the way these racial groups are presented in other analysis on voting rights—see Biggers and Hanmer 2017—and key in the rhetoric surrounding recent elections. For the period between 2000 and 2010, the data is derived from the official

Table 6.1 Descriptive Statistics of Race Variables

	Minimum	Maximum	Mean	Std. Deviation	N
Black	.31	37.59	10.663	9.611	864
Latino	.68	48.16	10.069	9.877	864

Source: Author.

Table 6.2   OLS Regression: Registered Voters per Polling Place and Race Variables

	Model 1 +	Model 2
Percent Black	6.238 (3.593)	4.340 (4.862)
Percent Latino	13.084* (3.390)	7.715 (4.532)
Population (Millions)		−11.427* (5.778)
Pop Density (Tens sq/Mile)		6.158** (1.457)
GDP per Capita (Thousands)		4.968 (4.153)
Spending Percent of GDP		−71.365** (14.927)
Year		97.412** (17.500)
West		130.706 (108.305)
South		7.488 (98.715)
Constant	1392.021* (66.693)	1493.518* (285.325)
Obs	298	298
R2	.046	.258
F	8.166*	12.503*

Source: Author.
**p value <.01; *p value <.05 + autocorrelation evident.

intercensal estimates produced by the US Census Bureau (US Census 2018b). For the remaining years, the five-year estimates are from the American Community Survey (US Census 2017). Initially we did an analysis using a percent of all minority populations in a state. While there was some significance to our findings, theoretically the percent of the black and Latino populations are more relevant and better measures.

These variables of race are first tested in restricted analyses on their own, then interacted with economic and partisan control terms, and finally placed in a fully constructed model with all effects together. The first of these analyses in table 6.2 is a simple OLS regression of the economic spending proxy on the two variables of interest.

Looking at table 6.3, Model 1 demonstrates the significance of the Latino population. However, Model 2, with the addition of controls, shows nonsignificance of both racial variables under evaluation. The coefficients on the control terms are also very much alike those in the early economics-only models, pointing toward a similarly limited influence of the primary race terms on the number of registered voters per polling place. It is at least encouraging that spending percent of GDP had a negative and significant coefficient in line with what would be expected, if the dependent variable is serving as a competent proxy.

In table 6.3, we examine the influence of race on the enactment of voter identification laws. In this analysis, the percentage of black population in the state has a significant coefficient with the expected sign. Therefore, the prediction of Hypothesis 8 that a proportionally greater black population would increase the odds of more restrictive voting laws is affirmed. Hypothesis 8b is not supported as the Latino variable is not significant. A crude comparison

Table 6.3 Ordered Logit: Voter ID Scale and Race Variables

	Model 1	Model 2
Percent Black	.046** (.007)	.033** (.011)
Percent Latino	.002 (.007)	−.010 (.012)
Population (Millions)		−.009 (.015)
Pop Density (Tens sq/Mile)		−.014** (.004)
GDP per Capita (Thousands)		−.030** (.010)
Spending Percent of GDP		−.336** (.039)
Year		.249** (.019)
West		−.140 (.242)
South		.536* (.220)
Obs	864	864
Chi-Square	46.248**	281.062**
Cox and Snell	.052	.278

Source: Author.
**p value <.01; *p value <.05.

Table 6.4 Ordinal Regression: Early Voting Scale and Race Variables

	Model 1	Model 2
Percent Black	−.050** (.007)	−.030** (.010)
Percent Latino	.021** (.006)	.013 (.009)
Population (Millions)		.031* (.012)
Pop Density (Tens sq/Mile)		−.016** (.003)
GDP per Capita (Thousands)		−.012 (.009)
Spending Percent of GDP		−.005 (.032)
Year		.033* (.016)
West		−.158 (.208)
South		−.617** (.207)
Obs	864	864
Chi-Square	82.235**	125.782**
Cox and Snell	.091	.135

Source: Author.
**p value <.01; *p value <.05. Standard errors in brackets.

with the equivalent economics and partisan restricted models (in tables 4.2 and 5.2, respectively) also revealed that the inclusion of race terms weakened the effect of Southern states. While a regional difference was still apparent and significant, it was reduced by almost half.

Table 6.4 is an ordinal regression of early voting laws on the race variables of interest. The results of Model 2 should be discussed with great caution, however, as it is the only model (with the control variables in this chapter) that fails a goodness of fit test. With this in mind, the significant result of this analysis was another confirmation of Hypothesis 8a—an increase in the black percentage of the population is met with a decrease in the odds of less restrictive voting laws being enacted.

Table 6.5   Binary Logistic Regression: Online Registration and Race Variables

	Model 1	Model 2
Percent Black	.008 (.009)	.076** (.020)
Percent Latino	.046** (.008)	.026 (.016)
Population (Millions)		−.026 (.021)
Pop Density (Tens sq/Mile)		−.004 (.005)
GDP per Capita (Thousands)		.016 (.014)
Spending Percent of GDP		−.169** (.053)
Year		.500** (.040)
West		2.105** (.385)
South		−.575 (.402)
Obs	864	864
Chi-Square	35.370**	408.439**
Constant	−1.844** (.169)	−7.640** (1.102)
Cox and Snell	.040	.377

**p value <.01. Standard errors in brackets.

Table 6.6   Ordinal Regression: Permanent Absentee Scale and Race Variables

	Model 1	Model 2
Percent Black	−.028** (.008)	.009 (.014)
Percent Latino	.024** (.007)	−.061** (.012)
Population (Millions)		.105** (.015)
Pop Density (Tens sq/Mile)		.018** (.004)
GDP per Capita (Thousands)		.027** (.011)
Spending Percent of GDP		.235** (.040)
Year		.000 (.020)
West		2.439** (.265)
South		−.421 (.288)
Obs	864	864
Chi-Square	24.578**	197.417**
Cox and Snell	.028	.204

**p value <.01. Standard errors in brackets.

Table 6.5 includes an examination of online registration laws. Contravening the expectation of Hypothesis 8a, the black percentage of the population is significant with a positive coefficient. In this restricted context, at least, proportionally high black populations seemed to increase the likelihood of nonrestrictive voting laws. Hypothesis 8b again lacked evidence.

Table 6.6 provides an ordinal regression of permanent absentee voting on the race and control variables. In Model 1, both race variables are significant but in Model 2, the percent black population loses significance with the inclusion of controls. Hypothesis 8b found support with Latino percentage of the population significantly reducing the odds of less restrictive voting laws.

Table 6.7 presents a fully restricted model centered on no-excuse absentee voting laws. The findings in this analysis are again in accord with the

Table 6.7 Binary Logistic Regression: No-Excuse Absentee and Race Variables

	Model 1	Model 2
Percent Black	−.097** (.010)	−.040** (.013)
Percent Latino	.040** (.009)	.026 (.017)
Population (Millions)		−.017 (.019)
Pop Density (Tens sq/Mile)		−.012** (.004)
GDP per Capita (Thousands)		−.029* (.013)
Spending Percent of GDP		−.055 (.044)
Year		.084** (.021)
West		1.660** (.315)
South		−.631* (.252)
Obs	864	864
Constant	.638** (.140)	1.650* (.785)
Chi-Square	170.869**	274.443**
Cox and Snell	.179	.272

**p value <.01. Standard errors in brackets.

anticipated results of Hypothesis 8. A rising black percentage of the population was met with steadily reducing odds of an unrestrictive voting law being enacted. However, assumptions regarding the Latino percent variable are again lacking in evidence. This is surprising given the significance of this analysis with partisan variables.

INTERACTIVE EFFECTS

This chapter evaluates the interactive effects of the three influences on voting barriers to determine the impact as a whole, and how they interact to shape limitations of voting rights. Claims of voter suppression, racial targeting, and partisan mischief have dominated most of the discussion about changes to the regulations that govern the casting of ballots through the electoral process. Throughout this book, we have suggested that these claims are largely rooted in the realities of the modern political system, a growing concern among key Republican voting demographics, and most especially the threat theory laid out in chapter 2. It provides the basis for much of our understanding and the best explanations at which we, and others, have arrived at.

Despite the seeming clarity of the role of the "threat" hypothesis in the development of voting access restrictions, or the strong evidence for the role of partisan protectionism (explored in the next chapter) in the development of these policies both in the current system and in the historical context, there remains a significant part of the modern Republican Party that seemingly lacks the circumstances for threat to be activated, and where partisan concerns are largely symbolic. Despite the current academic consensus on the role of race in these restrictions, there is at least some evidence that elected officials that support changes to voter access may take action for a multiplicity of reasons. Indeed, there exists a substantial and well-documented propensity for both parties to engage with election administration for explicitly and implicitly partisan reasons. Our own view suggests that while partisan and racial motivations are clearly active and likely the primary reason in the Republican Party's policy formulation in this area, there is likely to be something more going on in these policy implementations. This notion is heavily rooted in the traditional ideologies that underpin the coalition that is the modern Republican Party where different coalitions provide cover for other coalitions' motivations.

Thus, we believe that any examination of the motivations of policy that is not cognizant of this coalition and the resulting policy discussions and the ways in which the various parts of the coalition must appease each other lacks the explanatory power necessary to provide a cogent explanation of the motivations of the resulting policy. Given this belief, we seek to incorporate fiscal explanations with the more traditional explanations of race and partisanship in our exploration of electoral administration reforms.

Given our belief about the multiplicity of causes behind these decisions, we do not expect that fiscal concerns will be the dominant factor in any of our analyses. Rather we expect consistent with the literature—that there continues to be a strong partisan and racial impact that influences the passage of these restrictions. Rather we based on our understanding of the coalition that is the Republican Party, that these fiscal concerns are likely to be an active and important part of the story. After controlling for the partisan and racial effects, we expect to find that these fiscal concerns are an important part of the story that has been understudied at the peril of those who seek to expand voting access.

Table 6.8 provides the first set of interactive models, testing the relationship between race and economic terms. The addition of the economic terms and interactions to the models added very little multicollinearity. No main economic variables showed any significance, thus establishing no evidence for the predictions of the first three hypotheses. The only significant economic interaction term was that between black percentage of the population and change in revenue for the implementation of online registration. The implication of this term is that the odds of enacting less restrictive voting laws are jointly decreased by a rising black percentage of the population and a larger drop in expenditure. This finding provides a small piece of support for Hypothesis 1 and is in line with the suggestions of Hypothesis 8a.

Focusing on the primary subject of the chapter, the main race terms are significant in only three of the six models. Black percentage of the population had the expected significance and sign for voting identification laws (Model 2) but actually indicated a higher probability of less restrictive voting laws in

Table 6.8 Race and Economic Models

	Model 1 Registered Voters per Polling Place	Model 2 Voter ID	Model 3 Early Voting	Model 4 Online Reg	Model 5 Perm Absentee	Model 6 No-Excuse Absentee
Percent Black	6.017	.031*	-.024	.076**	.000	-.028
	(5.650)	(.013)	(.012)	(.021)	(.016)	(.016)
Percent Latino	6.204	-.021	.015	.012	-.061**	.042
	(5.255)	(.015)	(.012)	(.018)	(.014)	(.022)
Revenue Percent Change	4.152	-.010	.007	.066	.021	.007
	(13.212)	(.033)	(.028)	(.049)	(.034)	(.036)
Expenditure Percent Change	5.648	-.057	.032	-.044	-.063	.078
	(16.103)	(.037)	(.031)	(.055)	(.039)	(.042)
Population (Millions)	-10.345	-.011	.033**	-.024	.104**	-.016
	(5.886)	(.015)	(.013)	(.021)	(.016)	(.020)
Pop Density (Tens sq/Mile)	6.105**	-.014**	-.016**	-.002	.018**	-.012**
	(1.475)	(.004)	(.003)	(.005)	(.004)	(.004)
GDP per Capita (Thousands)	4.594	-.031**	-.012	.015	.028**	-.029*
	(4.299)	(.011)	(.010)	(.015)	(.011)	(.013)
Spending percent of GDP	-69.707**	-.340**	-.005	-.170**	.242**	-.064
	(15.391)	(.040)	(.033)	(.055)	(.041)	(.045)
Year	102.313**	.236**	.035*	.519**	-.005	.087**
	(18.659)	(.021)	(.017)	(.043)	(.022)	(.023)
West	138.015	-.130	-.150	2.113**	2.576**	1.740**
	(109.133)	(.246)	(.215)	(.392)	(.277)	(.333)
South	-7.006	.511*	-.666**	-.555	-.424	-.621**
	(100.634)	(.225)	(.214)	(.406)	(.297)	(.260)
Black * Revenue	.268	-.001	.000	-.006*	-.001	.002
	(.741)	(.002)	(.002)	(.003)	(.002)	(.002)
Black * Expenditure	-.345	.000	-.002	.001	.003	-.003
	(.798)	(.002)	(.002)	(.003)	(.002)	(.003)

(Continued)

Table 6.8 Race and Economic Models (*Continued*)

	Model 1 Registered Voters per Polling Place	Model 2 Voter ID	Model 3 Early Voting	Model 4 Online Reg	Model 5 Perm Absentee	Model 6 No-Excuse Absentee
Latino * Revenue	−.436	−.001	−.001	.000	−.001	.000
	(.776)	(.002)	(.002)	(.003)	(.002)	(.003)
Latino * Expenditure	.528	.003	.000	.004	.000	−.004
	(.819)	(.002)	(.002)	(.003)	(.002)	(.003)
Obs	298	816	816	816	816	816
Constant	1437.867**			−7.774**		1.313
	(295.050)			(1.131)		(.827)
Chi-Square		263.810**	124.564**	393.117**	198.447**	261.507**
R2	.249					
Cox and Snell		.276	.142	.382	.216	.274

Source: Author.
**p value <.01; *p value<.05. Standard errors in brackets.
Model 1 is an OLS regression; Models 2, 3, and 5 are ordinal regressions; Models 4 and 6 are Binary Logistic Regressions.

the context of online registration (Model 4). Latino percentage of the population is only significant for the enactment of permanent absentee voter laws (Model 5) but had the effect anticipated by Hypothesis 8b of reducing the odds of such laws being adopted.

The next set of interactive models in table 6.9 includes partisan control variables and their respective interactions with the two race terms. Much as in the prior models, the primary race terms had mixed results. The significant and positive coefficient for voter identification (Model 2) affirmed Hypothesis 8 and the significant and positive coefficient for online registration reversed the expectations of the same hypothesis. Latino percentage of the population had the expected effect for voter identification (Model 2) but was not significant in the other five models.

The three main partisan control terms fared collectively better in the combined model. In four of the six models, the significant terms had the expected effects of reducing the odds of less restrictive policy (although hypotheses regarding the effect of controlling any particular office are hampered by the variance in which offices are significant). However, for permanent absentee voting (Model 5) the significant effect for sole control of the office of chief election officer confounded expectations by indicating greater odds of unrestrictive policy. Taking the interactions between partisan control into account, a pattern emerges much like what was observed in the previous chapter. In the four models where these terms are significant, the cumulative effects of all partisan-only terms exhibited decreasing or even reversing returns to additional Republican control of state institutions.

Addressing the interactions between race and partisan control offers an even more complex array of results. Of the eleven significant interactions between the six models, seven accord with the predictions of Hypothesis 8a and 8b that a higher percentage of black and Latino populations will lead to higher odds of more restrictive policy. Four of the five models that do not are interactions between Latino percentage and Republican control, while only one black interaction term defies expectation, suggesting perhaps divergent political calculations regarding those two populations.

The final combined interaction models are presented in table 6.10. Economic interaction terms are not included in these models because of a lack of significance. As such, the only addition was of the main economic terms (changes in revenue and expenditure), which are universally nonsignificant themselves. This provided a final rebuke of the intimations of the first three hypotheses. No significant coefficients from the previous model were significantly altered, thus maintaining the previous findings regarding partisan control and race. The results of this test are clearer: we find statistically significant evidence for each of our larger hypotheses, and a strong impact of

Table 6.9 Race and Partisan Models

	Model 1 Registered Voters per Polling Place	Model 2 Voter ID	Model 3 Early Voting	Model 4 Online Reg	Model 5 Perm Absentee	Model 6 No-Excuse Absentee
Black	−7.489	.059**	−.026	.089*	−.004	.011
	(8.05)	(.017)	(.015)	(.035)	(.026)	(.023)
Latino	−9.832	.043*	.009	.045	.003	−.004
	(6.266)	(.019)	(.015)	(.024)	(.019)	(.024)
Rep Legislature	−189.573	−.465	−1.329**	−1.811*	.102	.135
	(172.47)	(.491)	(.389)	(.795)	(.467)	(.468)
Rep Governor	52.325	−.129	−1.300**	.520	−1.723**	−.339
	(167.208)	(.549)	(.377)	(.758)	(.510)	(.485)
Rep CEO	−309.982	2.979**	.107	−.529	1.121*	−1.292*
	(191.041)	(.523)	(.410)	(.902)	(.519)	(.579)
Population (Millions)	−14.943*	−.009	.062**	−.071*	.163**	.044
	(5.823)	(.023)	(.014)	(.028)	(.020)	(.026)
Pop Density (Tens sq/Mile)	4.018**	−.007	−.015**	−.010	.025**	−.011**
	(1.400)	(.004)	(.003)	(.006)	(.004)	(.004)
GDP per Capita (Thousands)	4.639	−.021	.022	−.006	−.045**	−.003
	(4.543)	(.013)	(.011)	(.020)	(.015)	(.017)
Spending Percent of GDP	−94.551**	−.325**	.104**	−.239**	.223**	.101
	(16.367)	(.054)	(.039)	(.065)	(.053)	(.056)
Year	108.956**	.247**	−.007	.614**	.046	.044
	(108.956)	(.025)	(.019)	(.057)	(.026)	(.027)
West	88.584	−1.193**	−.620*	2.368**	2.421**	1.768**
	(119.335)	(.317)	(.250)	(.518)	(.362)	(.418)
South	−97.673	.021	−1.418**	−.630	−1.821**	−1.717**
	(113.688)	(.298)	(.266)	(.528)	(.539)	(.355)
Rep Leg * Rep Gov	−440.725	2.989**	1.296*	−.508	−.566	1.527*
	(255.453)	(.672)	(.579)	(1.055)	(.739)	(.714)

	(1)	(2)	(3)	(4)	(5)	(6)
Rep Leg * Rep CEO	-249.76	-.677	2.772**	-.743	-.470	2.209**
	(223.682)	(.572)	(.529)	(1.067)	(.631)	(.718)
Rep Gov * Rep CEO	-569.695**	-.348	.430	-.437	1.178*	.626
	(202.896)	(.520)	(.415)	(.936)	(.560)	(.580)
Rep Leg * Rep Gov * Rep CEO	900.986**	-2.102*	-1.749*	1.114	-1.345	-1.682
	(331.963)	(.825)	(.722)	(1.450)	(.925)	(.960)
Black * Rep Leg	5.77	.053**	-.033	.022	-.008	-.082**
	(7.19)	(.020)	(.019)	(.037)	(.027)	(.026)
Black * Rep Gov	2.253	.019	.021	.023	.076**	.011
	(8.263)	(.020)	(.018)	(.039)	(.027)	(.026)
Black * Rep CEO	20.097*	-.059**	-.001	-.016	-.100**	.012
	(8.662)	(.022)	(.020)	(.042)	(.029)	(.029)
Latino * Rep Leg	4.033	.143**	-.022	.117**	.109**	-.044
	(8.841)	(.031)	(.020)	(.039)	(.026)	(.033)
Latino * Rep Gov	6.243	-.037	.053**	-.128**	.048*	.015
	(7.579)	(.026)	(.016)	(.032)	(.027)	(.027)
Latino * Rep CEO	24.612**	-.060	.008	.049	-.026	.039
	(9.364)	(.032)	(.018)	(.039)	(.024)	(.031)
Obs	259	756	756	756	756	756
Constant	2164.113**			-6.277**		-1.250
	(336.871)			(1.414)		(1.123)
Chi-Square		536.833**	203.497**	402.205**	252.751**	305.899**
R2	.386					
Cox and Snell		.508	.236	.413	.284	.333

Source: Author. Standard errors in brackets. *p value <.05 **p value <.01

Table 6.10 Interaction of Race, Economics, and Partisanship Models

	Model 1 Registered Voters per Polling Place	Model 2 Voter ID	Model 3 Early Voting	Model 4 Online Reg	Model 5 Perm Absentee	Model 6 No-Excuse Absentee
Black	-8.304	.059**	-.023	.089*	.005	.012
	(8.065)	(.017)	(.016)	(.035)	(.026)	(.024)
Latino	-9.652	.046*	.014	.045	.009	-.013
	(6.265)	(.019)	(.015)	(.025)	(.019)	(.025)
Rep Legislature	-192.129	-.549	-1.582**	-1.828*	.110	-.054
	(173.011)	(.502)	(.408)	(.798)	(.482)	(.489)
Rep Governor	53.447	.080	-1.417**	.553	-2.001**	-.420
	(168.125)	(.558)	(.395)	(.759)	(.545)	(.503)
Rep CEO	-345.002	3.065**	.304	-.497	1.185*	-1.315*
	(192.751)	(.539)	(.426)	(.906)	(.542)	(.614)
Revenue Percent Change	-3.945	-.030	.005	.008	.003	.029
	(7.575)	(.020)	(.017)	(.035)	(.023)	(.025)
Expend Percent Change	12.490	-.021	.007	-.018	-.029	.006
	(8.501)	(.022)	(.020)	(.035)	(.026)	(.028)
Population (Millions)	-14.337*	-.013	.064**	-.070*	.161**	.049
	(5.836)	(.024)	(.015)	(.028)	(.020)	(.028)
Pop Density (Tens sq/Mile)	3.980**	-.006	-.016**	-.010	.026**	-.010*
	(1.400)	(.004)	(.003)	(.006)	(.004)	(.004)
GDP per Capita (Thousands)	3.322	-.018	.022	-.005	-.041**	-.001
	(4.636)	(.013)	(.012)	(.020)	(.015)	(.018)
Spending Percent of GDP	-98.346**	-.318**	.107**	-.231**	.239**	.097
	(16.709)	(.056)	(.040)	(.066)	(.055)	(.057)
Year	112.929**	.229**	-.004	.610**	.040	.047
	(19.442)	(.027)	(.021)	(.057)	(.028)	(.029)
West	94.751	-1.155**	-.712**	2.374**	2.536**	1.985**
	(119.349)	(.328)	(.261)	(.518)	(.379)	(.454)

South	−106.012	−.139	−1.586**	−.617	−1.892**	−1.739**
	(113.777)	(.308)	(.279)	(.529)	(.373)	(.370)
Rep Leg * Rep Gov	−425.209	2.980**	1.357*	−.512	−.419	1.604*
	(255.735)	(.676)	(.599)	(1.054)	(.759)	(.722)
Rep Leg * Rep CEO	−212.048	−.839	2.839**	−.764	−.554	2.401**
	(225.360)	(.582)	(.545)	(1.069)	(.653)	(.749)
Rep Gov * Rep CEO	−553.098**	−.426	.299	−.456	1.362*	.828
	(203.128)	(.538)	(.432)	(.940)	(.584)	(.607)
Rep Leg * Rep Gov * Rep CEO	853.034*	−1.941*	−1.645*	1.136	−1.563	−1.913
	(333.368)	(.836)	(.743)	(1.452)	(.949)	(.984)
Black * Rep Leg	6.574	.059**	−.031	.022	−.005	−.075**
	(7.960)	(.020)	(.019)	(.037)	(.028)	(.027)
Black * Rep Gov	2.496	.012	.022	.022	.091**	.018
	(8.268)	(.021)	(.019)	(.039)	(.029)	(.027)
Black * Rep CEO	20.969*	−.063**	−.008	−.017	−.103**	.001
	(8.682)	(.023)	(.021)	(.043)	(.031)	(.029)
Latino * Rep Leg	2.843	.158**	−.019	.118**	.119**	−.034
	(8.880)	(.032)	(.020)	(.039)	(.026)	(.034)
Latino * Rep Gov	6.980	−.052*	.058**	−.129**	.054*	.019
	(7.621)	(.027)	(.017)	(.032)	(.023)	(.028)
Latino * Rep CEO	24.044*	−.048	−.009	.050	−.034	.032
	(9.381)	(.033)	(.019)	(.039)	(.025)	(.033)
Obs	259	714	714	714	714	714
Constant	2212.068**			−6.359**		−1.415
	(343.961)			(1.430)		(1.169)
Chi-Square		520.835**	208.958**	380.608**	250.953**	292.017**
R2	.387					
Cox and Snell		.518	.254	.413	.296	.336

Source: Author. Standard errors in brackets. *p value < .05 **p value < .01

race (black percentage) on the ordered scale. Likewise, our fiscal and partisan measures were similarly important predictors.

CONCLUSION

As we have traced throughout this chapter the role of race in the decision to adopt more restrictive voting access rules, it has been and continues to be a prominent one, and one that persists even in the face of countervailing political or economic pressures. This clear racial impact has many potential sources, but most clearly, it represents the threat response from elected officials as they attempt to engage the political process to their own advantage. This is most clearly illustrated by the sign change on each of the racial measures between the measures squared term. This flip illustrates that at some point the risk calculation for voting access restrictions flips and the potential costs of adopting these restrictions outweigh the political benefits and, as a result, elected officials are able to respond to the changing demographics with changes in policy, as would be expected if they are updating to new information as predicted.

While this chapter has focused primarily on the racial origins of these restrictions, the empirical test we illustrate here provides strong evidence that the decisions to restrict voting access are the result of a multiplicity of causes, including race, and further study is both warranted and necessary to better parse out this impact over a larger time period.

As we have noted across this book, and in this chapter in particular, we were skeptical of the claims made by a vocal minority that the root cause of voting access restrictions was simple racial animus. As we have noted, our skepticism is in large part borne of our interaction with and close relationship with numerous elected officials, policymakers, and others. However, this book's examination has clarified the role of race in these sorts of decisions. We now view race as a key part of the policy debate and interplay as the public policy process works itself out as it always does, messily and over longer periods than we might want, and the current period is one such messy time. We find that race has a significant and substantive impact on the decisions to implement voting barriers. Race, along with partisanship and economic conditions, in this analysis illustrated the complex interplay that has come to impact public policy.

Chapter 7

What's Next?

Policy Implications

WHAT WE FOUND . . .

We set out with the expectations to find a linkage and causality between economic factors of the Great Recession and voting restrictions post-2008. What we found was not supportive of that expectation. While the initial results supported Hypotheses 1–3 that examined spending and revenue factors, further analysis limited those findings, particularly when looking at the context of other key independent variables like race and partisanship. Looking at the partisan variables there is some support (at least when investigated alone) for partisan motivation for voting laws. While these were unsupportive of Hypothesis 7 all of our other partisan hypotheses found some support—particularly Hypothesis 4 which looks at the Republican control of the legislature. However, in chapter 6 we see the biggest impact on our findings. The significance of the black population in the models demonstrates the underlying connection to racial factors. So what does this mean? From the start it demonstrates that the expected relationship between fiscal factors and the enactment of voting laws did not follow our expectation. We posited in chapter 3 that this may be the change in burden from the state to the voter but perhaps as government spending decreased, elections were generally spared from cost cutting (and perhaps even invested in more when it came to online registration).

It is important to note that as we added factors into the interaction models, none of the economic variables were significant in any of the models and there was an increase in the significance of the racial variables. This provides credence to our theory which suggests that utilizing fiscal conservatism serves as a "Baptist" to protect the actions of the "Bootleggers" and allows voting suppression in states where there are high populations of blacks and

Latinos. The findings are not necessarily novel but set in the context of the policy imperatives facing state governments and election officials and demonstrate how these tactics may be sold to fiscal conservative members of the Republican Party.

SO WHAT?

In 2018, the United States had the highest turnout for a midterm election (see table 7.1). So why do we care about voter suppression activities and what caused them? Well, voter suppression does happen—even if turnout increased. Imagine what the turnout would be if there had not been voter suppression tactics like voter identification, and had early voting or no-fault absentee voting been available. Simply because the numbers went up does not mean we should not be paying attention to these policies and their causes. The number of quotes from politicians provided in this book illustrates simply that some want to continue to suppress votes and will continue to act to do so. Whether this suppression is intentional or a by-product of other actions, the impact is clear (Berke 2018). As noted in Berke (2018), voter suppression is an American tradition and with the increased perception of threat—be it economic, partisan, or race. The desire to maintain one's place in the world puts emphasis on continuing voter suppression of "others." Will this hold for 2020? In the eloquent words of Sarah Palin—*you betcha!* With the presidency, potentially additional Supreme Court seats, control of Congress on the line, as well as various state offices, an increased threat is felt to politicians and voters alike.

WHO IS TURNING OUT?

Research has shown that there was an increase in voter turnout of racial minorities' post-enactment of the VRA in 1965. They also show that there was a sharp decline in the turnout of racial minorities' post-*Shelby* (Ang 2019). However, these rebounded for the most part in 2018 (see figure 7.1). Well, the political climate of the 2016 election demonstrated that there was a desire to participate regardless of the barriers in place. Ironically, the threats led to increased barriers through election policy and spending also served as a motivation for groups who felt threatened to turn out to vote.

Participation among African American voters decreased almost 8 percent between 2012 and 2016. Much of that was driven by the difference in presidential candidates between 2012 and 2016, candidates that were not as motivated to get out to vote among the African American community. However,

Table 7.1 Changes in Voter Turnout

State	2018 VEP Turnout (%)	2018–2014 VEP Change (%)	2014 VEP Turnout (%)	2014–2010 VEP Change (%)	2010 VEP Turnout (%)	2010–2006 VEP Change (%)	2006 VEP Turnout (%)
United States	50.30%	13.60%	36.70%	−5.10%	41.80%	0.50%	41.30%
Alabama	47.30%	14.10%	33.20%	−10.10%	43.30%	5.80%	37.50%
Alaska	54.60%	−0.20%	54.80%	1.90%	52.90%	1.70%	51.20%
Arizona	49.10%	15.00%	34.10%	−7.50%	41.60%	2.00%	39.60%
Arkansas	41.40%	1.10%	40.30%	2.40%	37.90%	−1.00%	38.90%
California	49.60%	18.90%	30.70%	−15.20%	45.90%	4.70%	41.20%
Colorado	63.00%	8.30%	54.70%	3.00%	51.70%	3.60%	48.10%
Connecticut	54.40%	11.90%	42.50%	−3.40%	45.90%	−1.80%	47.70%
Delaware	51.40%	16.50%	34.90%	−14.10%	49.00%	6.10%	42.90%
District of Columbia	43.70%	8.00%	35.70%	6.10%	29.60%	0.90%	28.70%
Florida	54.90%	11.60%	43.30%	1.10%	42.20%	2.10%	40.10%
Georgia	55.00	16.40	38.60	−2.00	40.60	5.50	35.10
Hawaii	39.30	2.80	36.50	−3.80	40.30	1.90	38.40
Idaho	50.00	10.20	39.80	−3.10	42.90	−3.30	46.20
Illinois	51.40	10.60	40.80	−2.30	43.10	1.70	41.40
Indiana	46.90	18.20	28.70	−9.40	38.10	0.40	37.70
Iowa	57.70	7.40	50.30	−0.40	50.70	1.50	49.20
Kansas	51.20	7.90	43.30	0.70	42.60	−1.70	44.30
Kentucky	48.60	3.70	44.90	0.60	44.30	0.10	44.20
Louisiana	44.80	−0.10	44.90	4.90	40.00	8.60	31.40
Maine	60.20	1.50	58.70	2.80	55.90	1.70	54.20
Maryland	54.20	12.20	42.00	−4.70	46.70	−0.50	47.20
Massachusetts	54.60	9.90	44.70	−4.70	49.40	0.10	49.30
Michigan	57.80	14.60	43.20	−1.90	45.10	−7.70	52.80
Minnesota	64.20	13.60	50.60	−5.20	55.80	−4.70	60.50
Mississippi	42.70	13.70	29.00	−8.00	37.00	7.60	29.40

(Continued)

Table 7.1 Changes in Voter Turnout (*Continued*)

State	2018 VEP Turnout (%)	2018–2014 VEP Change (%)	2014 VEP Turnout (%)	2014–2010 VEP Change (%)	2010 VEP Turnout (%)	2010–2006 VEP Change (%)	2006 VEP Turnout (%)
Missouri	53.40	19.80	33.60	−12.10	45.70	−5.50	51.20
Montana	62.00	14.50	47.50	−0.90	48.40	−8.70	57.10
Nebraska	51.80	10.40	41.40	2.70	38.70	−10.10	48.80
Nevada	47.50	17.90	29.60	−11.80	41.40	4.30	37.10
New Hampshire	54.60	6.30	48.30	2.20	46.10	3.20	42.90
New Jersey	53.10	20.60	32.50	−5.20	37.70	−2.90	40.60
New Mexico	47.30	11.90	35.40	−9.30	44.70	1.60	43.10
New York	45.20	16.20	29.00	−7.30	36.30	−0.20	36.50
North Carolina	49.60	8.40	41.20	1.40	39.80	7.30	32.50
North Dakota	58.60	13.60	45.00	−1.60	46.60	1.20	45.40
Ohio	50.90	14.70	36.20	−10.00	46.20	−3.30	49.50
Oklahoma	42.50	12.50	30.00	−9.10	39.10	2.70	36.40
Oregon	61.50	8.10	53.40	−0.50	53.90	0.70	53.20
Pennsylvania	51.40	14.90	36.50	−5.90	42.40	−1.70	44.10
Rhode Island	48.10	5.70	42.40	−3.00	45.40	−6.70	52.10
South Carolina	45.20	10.00	35.20	−5.10	40.30	4.90	35.40
South Dakota	53.30	8.60	44.70	−9.20	53.90	−4.90	58.80
Tennessee	45.10	15.30	29.80	−5.30	35.10	−7.00	42.10
Texas	46.30	18.00	28.30	−4.40	32.70	1.80	30.90
Utah	52.00	21.70	30.30	−6.50	36.80	1.80	35.00
Vermont	55.90	15.10	40.80	−9.00	49.80	−5.20	55.00
Virginia	54.80	18.00	36.80	−2.30	39.10	−5.40	44.50
Washington	58.90	15.80	43.10	−11.20	54.30	7.00	47.30
West Virginia	42.50	10.50	32.00	−5.20	37.20	3.40	33.80
Wisconsin	61.70	4.80	56.90	4.50	52.40	−1.30	53.70
Wyoming	48.70	9.00	39.70	−6.30	46.00	−5.80	51.80

Source: United States Election Project.

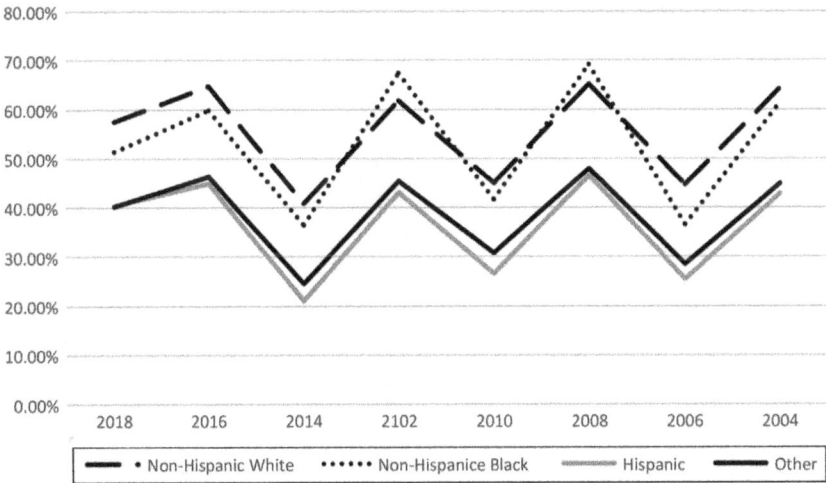

Figure 7.1 VEP Turnout by Race or Ethnicity. Author generated using date from Ang 2018.

there was also a decrease in the midterm elections from 2010 to 2014, which mostly disappeared in 2018. The motivation to turn out in 2018 must be couched in the context of policy enactment and rhetoric of the administration. Regardless, a story needs to be told about the change in electoral turnout for minority voters even in the face of voter suppression tactics.

NEXT STEPS?

As this manuscript was being prepared, we saw countless examples of rhetoric in the media that confirmed the findings of this manuscript. "Send them back," "Shitholes," and "disgusting, rat and rodent infested mess" provide examples about how the overt message is being sent to voters and supporters. However, it is the covert, more nuanced messages that we ought to be aware of as politicians use fiscal conservatism to hide the intent of policy and have lasting repercussions.

Perhaps this book is premature regarding the full extent of the motivations surrounding these tactics and the next twenty years will tell us the true impact of recessions, partisanship, and race on electoral access. However, there is a story here to demonstrate how these three factors contribute to the circumstances of today. While not outlandish, future studies may want to collect and look at precinct-level data to evaluate the individual cost per voter and how that has changed post-2008.

Appendix 1

Table A.1   **Changes to Voter Laws by State**

State/Law	Law Type	Year Enacted
Alabama		
No law needed.	Online Registration	
Act 673	Voter ID (Non-strict, photo)	2011
HB 193	Voter ID (Non-strict, non-photo)	2003
Alaska		
No law needed.	Online Registration	2015
Arizona		
SB 1074	Early Voting (sixteen to thirty days before)	2009
SB 1053	Early Voting (more than thirty days before)	2008
HB 2102	Permanent Absentee (Full)	2007
Proposition 200	Voter ID (Strict, non-photo)	2004
No law needed.	Online Registration	2002
Arkansas		
Act 633	Voter ID (Non-strict, photo)	2017
Courts struck down law.	Voter ID (None)	2014
Act 595	Voter ID (Strict, photo)	2013
California		
SB 397	Online Registration	2011
AB 1520	Permanent Absentee (Full)	2001
Colorado		
HB 1303	Mail ballot elections	2013
HB 1160	Online Registration	2009
SB 102	Voter ID (Non-strict, non-photo)	2003
Connecticut		
HB 5024	Online Registration	2012
PA 173	Permanent Absentee (Partial)	2011
HB 6634	Voter ID (Non-strict, non-photo)	2001
Delaware		
No law needed.	Online Registration	2014

(Continued)

Table A.1   Changes to Voter Laws by State (Continued)

State/Law	Law Type	Year Enacted
Florida		
SB 228	Online Registration	2015
SB 1118	No-excuse Absentee	2001
Georgia		
SB 92	Online Registration	2012
HB 92	Early Voting (sixteen to thirty days before)	2011
HB 244	Voter ID (Strict, photo)	2005
HB 244	No-excuse Absentee	2005
Hawaii		
HB 1755	Online Registration	2012
SB 156	Permanent Absentee (Full)	2008
Idaho		
SB 1297	Online Registration	2016
HB 107	Early Voting (sixteen to thirty days before)	2013
HB 496	Voter ID (Non-strict, photo)	2010
Illinois		
SB 172	Early Voting (more than thirty days before)	2015
HB 2418	Online Registration	2013
HB 1560	Early Voting (one to fifteen days before)	2013
SB 2002	No-Excuse Absentee	2009
HB 1968	Early Voting (sixteen to thirty days before)	2005
Indiana		
HB 1346	Online Registration	2009
SB 483	Voter ID (Strict, photo)	2005
Iowa		
HB 516	Voter ID (Non-strict, non-photo)	2017
No law needed.	Online Registration	2016
Kansas		
Act 56	Voter ID (Strict, photo)	2011
No law needed.	Online Registration	2009
Kentucky		
No law needed.	Online Registration	2016
Louisiana		
HB 520	Online Registration	2009
Maryland		
HB 740	Online Registration	2011
Massachusetts		
HB 3788	Online Registration	2014
HB 3788	Early Voting (one to fifteen days before)	2014
Minnesota		
SB 455	Early Voting (more than thirty days before)	2015
HB 3788	Online Registration	2014
Implemented before law.	Online Registration	2013
HB 894	No-excuse Absentee	2013
HB 894	Permanent Absentee (Full)	2013
Mississippi		
Act 526	Voter ID (Strict, Photo)	2012

(Continued)

Table A.1   Changes to Voter Laws by State (Continued)

State/Law	Law Type	Year Enacted
Missouri		
Courts struck down law.	Voter ID (Non-strict, non-photo)	2007
SB 1014	Voter ID (Strict, Photo)	2006
SB 675	Voter ID (Non-strict, non-photo)	2002
Montana		
SB 88	Permanent Absentee (Full)	2005
HB 190	Voter ID (Non-strict, non-photo)	2003
Nebraska		
LB 661	Online Registration	2014
Nevada		
SB 447	Permanent Absentee (Full)	2017
AB 82	Online Registration	2011
New Hampshire		
Act 284	Voter ID (Non-strict, photo)	2012
New Jersey		
SB 1380	No-Excuse Absentee	2009
SB 1380	Permanent Absentee (Full)	2009
New Mexico		
SB 643	Online Registration	2015
New York		
No law needed.	Online Registration	2011
North Carolina		
HB 836	Voter ID (Non-strict, photo)	2015
HB 589	Voter ID (Strict, photo)	2013
HB 977	No-Excuse Absentee	2001
North Dakota		
§ 16.1-01-04 Amended	Voter ID (Strict, non-photo)	2017
HB 1332	Voter ID (Strict, photo)	2015
Act 167	Voter ID (Non-strict, photo)	2013
SB 2248	Early Voting (one to fifteen days before)	2003
SB 2394	Voter ID (Non-strict, non-photo)	2003
Ohio		
SB 63	Online Registration	2016
SB 238	Early Voting (sixteen to thirty days before)	2013
HB 3	Voter ID (Strict, non-photo)	2006
Oklahoma		
SB 313	Online Registration	2015
Question 749	Voter ID (Non-strict, non-photo)	2010
Oregon		
HB 2386	Online Registration	2009
Pennsylvania		
No law needed.	Online Registration	2015
Courts struck down law.	Voter ID (None)	2014
Act 18	Voter ID (Strict, photo)	2012
Rhode Island		
SB 2513	Online Registration	2016
Act 2011-201/199	Voter ID (Non-strict, photo)	2014
Phase 2		

(Continued)

Table A.1 Changes to Voter Laws by State (Continued)

State/Law	Law Type	Year Enacted
Act 2011-201/199 Phase 1	Voter ID (Non-strict, non-photo)	2011
South Carolina		
HB 4945	Online Registration	2012
South Dakota		
HB 1176	Voter ID (Non-strict, photo)	2003
Tennessee		
SB 1626	Online Registration	2016
Act 323	Voter ID (Strict, photo)	2011
Texas		
§ 6-63-001 Amended	Voter ID (Non-strict, photo)	2017
Act 123	Voter ID (Strict, photo)	2011
HB 1549	Voter ID (Strict, non-photo)	2003
Utah		
SB 25	Online Registration	2009
HB 126	Voter ID (Non-strict, non-photo)	2009
HB 15	Early Voting (one to fifteen days before)	2006
HB 9	No-Excuse Absentee	2004
Vermont		
No law needed.	Online Registration	2015
Virginia		
HB 1337	Voter ID (Strict, photo)	2013
HB 2341	Online Registration	2013
HB 9	Voter ID (Strict, non-photo)	2012
Washington		
HB 1528	Online Registration	2007
SB 5499	Voter ID (Non-strict, non-photo)	2005
	Mail ballot elections	2005
West Virginia		
§3-1-34 and §3-1-41	Voter ID (Non-strict, non-photo)	2016
SB 477	Online Registration	2013
SB 581	Early Voting (one to fifteen days before)	2011
Wisconsin		
SB 295	Online Registration	2016
Act 23	Voter ID (Strict, photo)	2011

Source: Compiled by the contributors and author.

Appendix 2

Table A.2 State Financial Expenditures during Elections

Category	State	Details
State pays all expenses for federal or state elections.	Alaska	State pays for federal and state elections and for certain local elections.
	Delaware	The State Department of Elections pays for all election administration in the state.
State pays all expenses if only state candidates or issues are on the ballot. If other local issues are also on the ballot, state pays a portion of election expenses.	Alabama	State pays for half of elections when there are county races or an election to amend the constitution on the ballot. The state pays for the total cost of an election when the election is only for federal or state offices.
	Colorado	State reimburses counties for all election costs if the only item on the ballot is a statewide ballot issue. For any election where there is a statewide ballot issue/question on the ballot, the state reimburses at 90 cents per active registered voter in counties with 100,000 or fewer registered voters, or 80 cents per voter in counties with more than 100,000 voters.
	Hawaii	State pays all expenses for state elections. When both state and county offices are on the ballot, counties pay a prorated amount based on the number of registered voters and the state pays remaining expenses.
	Louisiana	State pays for election expenses during gubernatorial and congressional general, primary elections, and presidential primary elections, unless local candidates or questions also appear on the ballot, in which case the state pays half. The remaining half is split between the state and local or municipal jurisdictions participating in the election.

(Continued)

123

Table A.2   State Financial Expenditures during Elections (Continued)

Category	State	Details
State bears a portion of the cost of all elections.	Kentucky	State reimburses counties for the cost of elections at a set rate of $255 per precinct annually.
	Rhode Island	Local jurisdictions pay for poll workers and polling sites. The state bears all other costs of the election, such as voting equipment, polling place supplies, and ballots.
State pays for statewide special elections or statewide elections that do not coincide with regularly scheduled elections when there is only a state candidate or question on the ballot. If other local issues are also on the ballot, state may pay a portion of election expenses.	Arkansas	The state reimburses counties for statewide special elections and nonpartisan general elections on an estimated average cost per voter.
	Florida	State reimburses the actual expenses of holding a statewide special election.
	Iowa	State reimburses for special elections of constitutional amendments or statewide public measures that are not held at the same time as the general election.
	Michigan	State reimburses for actual costs of statewide special elections.
	Missouri	State pays for statewide elections when only state questions or candidates are on the ballot. State reimburses localities for the cost of conducting statewide elections in off-years. State shares a proportional cost of elections when state questions or candidates are on the same ballot as those from other political subdivisions.
	North Dakota	State pays expenses for special elections held to fill vacancies in the Senate or General Assembly.
	Ohio	State pays for the entire cost of an election when a statewide ballot measure is the only election on the ballot. When there is both a constitutional amendment from the state and ballot measures from a political subdivision, the state pays a proportional division of costs. State pays for special elections in certain instances.
	Oregon	State pays for special elections, statewide recall or other statewide special elections not regularly scheduled. There is a mechanism for county reimbursement, if they are in fiscal distress.

(Continued)

Table A.2   State Financial Expenditures during Elections (Continued)

Category	State	Details
	Pennsylvania	State reimburses county boards of elections for those additional costs incurred in any special election held to fill a vacancy in the General Assembly.
	Tennessee	State reimburses for all expenses for special elections when only a state assembly member is on the ballot.
	Washington	State reimburses prorated share of costs when state officers or measures are voted on in a state primary or general election in an odd-number year, and for a vacancy election to fill the position of US senator or representative.
	West Virginia	State reimburses for reasonable expenses for special elections to fill a vacancy.
State pays for statewide primary and presidential primary elections.	Arkansas	State reimburses counties for presidential primary elections and statewide primary elections on an estimated average cost per voter basis.
	South Carolina	State pays all costs associated with primaries for state offices, offices including more than one county, countywide offices and special district offices. State conducts and pays for presidential preference primaries. Political parties may charge filing fees for each candidate certified to appear on the presidential primary ballot.
	Texas	State reimburses localities for the majority of costs of all primary elections.
State pays for presidential primary elections	Arizona	State reimburses counties for presidential primary elections at the rate of $1.25 per active registered voter.
	Idaho	State reimburses all costs related to a presidential primary.
	Kansas	State reimburses counties for direct expenses of a presidential preference primary election.
	Michigan	State reimburses localities for actual costs of presidential primaries.
	Minnesota	The Secretary of State reimburses counties and municipalities for expenses incurred in the administration of the presidential nomination primary.

(Continued)

Table A.2 State Financial Expenditures during Elections (Continued)

Category	State	Details
	Missouri	State pays for all costs of presidential preference primaries unless there are political subdivisions holding an election on the same day, in which case the cost is proportional.
	Tennessee	State reimburses all expenses for presidential preferences primaries.
	Virginia	State pays for presidential primary elections.
	Washington	State reimburses all costs associated with a presidential primary election if it is held alone, and a prorated share of the costs otherwise.

Source: NCSL 2018a.

Bibliography

127 Congressional Record H6986-87 (daily ed. Oct. 2, 1981).

Abrajano, Marisa, and Zoltan L. Hajnal. 2015. *White Backlash: Immigration, Race, and American Politics*. Princeton, NJ: Princeton University Press.

Abramowitz, Alan I. "Partisan redistricting and the 1982 congressional elections." *The Journal of Politics* 45, no. 3 (1983): 767–770.

Abramowitz, Alan I. "Incumbency, campaign spending, and the decline of competition in US House elections." *The Journal of Politics* 53, no. 1 (1991): 34–56.

Abramowitz, Alan I., Brad Alexander, and Matthew Gunning. "Incumbency, redistricting, and the decline of competition in US House elections." *The Journal of Politics* 68, no. 1 (2006): 75–88.

Aldrich, John H. "Presidential address: Southern parties in state and nation." *The Journal of Politics* 62, no. 3 (2000): 643–670.

Allport, Gordon W. 1954. *The Nature of Prejudice*. Reading, MA: Addison Publishing.

Alvarez, R. M. L., S. Ansolabehere, and C. H. Wilson. 2002. "Election day voter registration in the United States: How one-step voting can change the composition of the American electorate." Caltech/MIT Voting Technology Project Working Paper.

Alvarez, R. Michael, Thad E. Hall, Ines Levin, and Charles Stewart III. "Voter opinions about election reform: Do they support making voting more convenient?" *Election Law Journal* 10, no. 2 (2011): 73–87.

Anderson, Jonathan. 2018. "Green Bay won't expand early voting this year." *Green Bay Press Gazette*. https://www.greenbaypressgazette.com/story/news/2018/03/02/green-bay-wont-expand-early-voting-year/384984002/.

Ang, D. "Do 40-year-old facts still matter? Long-run effects of federal oversight under the voting rights act." *American Economic Journal: Applied Economics* 11, no. 3 (2019): 1–53.

Ansolabehere, Stephen, Nathaniel Persily, and Charles Stewart III. "Race, religion, and vote choice in the 2008 election: Implications for the future of the Voting Rights Act." *Harvard Law Review* 123 (2009): 1385.

Arceneaux, Kevin and Stephen P. Nicholson. "Who wants to have a tea party? The who, what, and why of the Tea Party movement." *PS: Political Science & Politics* 45, no. 4 (2012): 700–710.

Arnosti, Nathan, and Michael A. Pagano. 2018. "How the 2018 election reshaped state and local governments' fiscal policy space." *Brookings Institute*, November 27, 2018. https://www.brookings.edu/research/how-the-2018-elections-reshape d-state-and-local-governments-fiscal-policy-space/.

Ashmore, Richard D., and Frances K. Del Boca. 1976. "Psychological approaches to understanding intergroup conflicts." In *Towards the Elimination of Racism*, pp. 73–123.

Atkeson, Lonna Rae, R. Michael Alvarez, Thad E. Hall, and J. Andrew Sinclair. "Balancing fraud prevention and electoral participation: Attitudes toward voter identification." *Social Science Quarterly* 95, no. 5 (2014): 1381–1398.

Atkeson, Lonna Rae, Lisa Ann Bryant, Thad E. Hall, Kyle Saunders, and Michael Alvarez. "A new barrier to participation: Heterogeneous application of voter identification policies." *Electoral Studies* 29, no. 1 (2010): 66–73.

Augoustinos, Martha, and Danielle Every. "The language of 'race' and prejudice: A discourse of denial, reason, and liberal-practical politics." *Journal of Language and Social Psychology* 26, no. 2 (2007): 123–141.

Baker v. Carr 369 US 186 (1962).

Baird, Addy. 2018. "Why the 'blue wave' might not save democrats in the senate." *Think Progress*, October 15, 2018. https://thinkprogress.org/blue-wave-house-vs-senate-forecasts-2962699c461e/.

Baqir, Reza. "Districting and government overspending." *Journal of Political Economy* 110, no. 6 (2002): 1318–1354.

Barreto, Matt A., Stephen A. Nuno, and Gabriel R. Sanchez. 2007. "Voter ID requirements and the disenfranchisements of Latino, Black and Asian voters." In *Annual Meeting of the American Political Science Association*, Chicago, Illinois, vol. 30.

Barrilleaux, Charles J., and Mark E. Miller. "The political economy of state Medicaid policy." *American Political Science Review* 82, no. 4 (1988): 1089–1107.

Behrens, Angela, Christopher Uggen, and Jeff Manza. "Ballot manipulation and the "menace of Negro domination": Racial threat and felon disenfranchisement in the United States, 1850–2002." *American Journal of Sociology* 109, no. 3 (2003): 559–605.

Berinsky, Adam J. "The perverse consequences of electoral reform in the United States." *American Politics Research* 33, no. 4 (2005): 471–491.

Berke, Lauren Simkin. 2018. "Vote. That's just what they don't want you to do." *The New York Times*, March 10, 2018.

Berman, Ari. 2016. "Welcome to the First Presidential Elections since the Voting Rights Act was Gutted." https://www.rollingstone.com/politics/politics-news/wel come-to-the-first-presidential-election-since-voting-rights-act-gutted-179737/.

Besley, Timothy, and Anne Case. "Political institutions and policy choices: Evidence from the United States." *Journal of Economic Literature* 41, no. 1 (2003): 7–73.

Biggers, Daniel R., and Michael J. Hanmer. "Understanding the adoption of voter identification laws in the American states." *American Politics Research* 45, no. 4 (2017): 560–588.

Blais, Andre, Donald Blake, and Stephane Dion. "Do parties make a difference? Parties and the size of government in liberal democracies." *American Journal of Political Science* 37, no. 1 (1993): 40–62.

Bloch, Katrina Rebecca. "'Anyone can be an illegal': Color-blind ideology and maintaining Latino/Citizen borders." *Critical Sociology* 40, no. 1 (2014): 47–65.

Bonilla-Silva, Eduardo. "The linguistics of color blind racism: How to talk nasty about Blacks without sounding 'racist'." *Critical Sociology* 28, nos. 1–2 (2002): 41–64.

Bonilla-Silva, E. 2013. *Racism without Racists: Color-blind Racism and the Persistence of Racial Inequality in America.* Lanham, MD: Rowman & Littlefield.

Bonilla-Silva, Eduardo, and Tyrone A. Forman. "'I am not a Racist but …': Mapping White College Students' racial ideology in the USA." *Discourse & Society* 11, no. 1 (2000): 50–85.

Bowler, Shaun, and Todd Donovan. "A partisan model of electoral reform: Voter identification laws and confidence in state elections." *State Politics & Policy Quarterly* 16, no. 3 (2016): 340–361.

Bowler, Shaun, and Todd Donovan. "Partisan predispositions and public support for making it easier to vote." *American Politics Research* 46, no. 6 (2018): 971–995.

Boyd, Thomas M., and Stephen J. Markman. "The 1982 amendments to the voting rights act: A legislative history." *Washington and Lee Law Review* 40, no. 3 (1983): 1347–1428.

Brady, David W., and Craig Volden. *Revolving Gridlock: Politics and Policy from Carter to Clinton.* Boulder, CO: Westview Press, 1998.

Bradner, Eric. "Mississippi's US Senate race comes to a close amid racial controversies." *CNN.* https://www.cnn.com/2018/11/27/politics/mississippi-senate-runoff -election/index.html.

Brettell, Caroline B., and Faith G. Nibbs. "Immigrant suburban settlement and the 'threat' to middle class status and identity: The case of farmers branch, Texas." *International Migration* 49, no. 1 (2011): 1–30.

Buchanan, Robert J., Joseph C. Cappelleri, and Robert L. Ohsfeldt. "The social environment and Medicaid expenditures: Factors influencing the level of state Medicaid spending." *Public Administration Review* 51, no. 1 (1991): 67–73.

Burch, Traci. "Did disfranchisement laws help elect President Bush? New evidence on the turnout rates and candidate preferences of Florida's ex-felons." *Political Behavior* 34, no. 1 (2012): 1–26.

Burkhardt, Brett C. "Ideology over strategy: Extending voting rights to felons and ex-felons, 1966–1992." *The Social Science Journal* 48, no. 2 (2011): 356–363.

Cain, Bruce E. "Assessing the partisan effects of redistricting." *American Political Science Review* 79, no. 2 (1985): 320–333.

Cain, Bruce E. "Moving past section 5: More fingers or a new dike?" *Election Law Journal* 12, no. 3 (2013): 338–340.

Cain, Bruce E., and Janet C. Campagna. "Predicting partisan redistricting disputes." *Legislative Studies Quarterly* 12, no. 2 (1987): 265–274.

Carson, Jamie L., Michael H. Crespin, Charles J. Finocchiaro, and David W. Rohde. "Redistricting and party polarization in the US House of Representatives." *American Politics Research* 35, no. 6 (2007): 878–904.

Clarke, Monet. "Race, partisanship, and the Voting Rights Act (VRA): African–Americans in Texas from reconstruction to the republican redistricting of 2004." *Texas Journal on Civil Liberties & Civil Rights* 10 (2004): 223.

Colby, Sandra L., and Jennifer M. Ortman. 2014. "Projections of the size and composition of the U.S. population: 2014 to 2060." *Current Population Reports*, P25-1143, U.S. Census Bureau, Washington, DC.

Congressional Budget Office. *Douglas W. Elmendorf letter to Senator Charles E. Grassley*, March 2, 2009.

Conn, Jason Belmont. "Felon disenfranchisement laws: Partisan politics in the legislatures." *Michigan Journal of Race & Law* 10 (2004): 495.

Cox, Adam B., and Richard T. Holden. "Reconsidering racial and partisan gerrymandering." *University of Chicago Law Review* 78 (2011): 553.

Cox Gary, W., and Mathew D. McCubbins. 1993. *Legislative Leviathan: Party Government in the House*. Boston, MA: Cambridge University Pres.

Cox, Gary W., and Mathew D. McCubbins. 2005. *Setting the Agenda: Responsible Party Government in the US House of Representatives*. Cambridge University Press.

Davis, Ronald. n.d. "Creating Jim crow: In-depth essay." https://www.hatboro-horsham.org/cms/lib2/PA01000027/Centricity/Domain/374/Jim_Crow_Era-Lynching.pdf.

Dawson, Richard E., and James A. Robinson. "Inter-party competition, economic variables, and welfare policies in the American states." *The Journal of Politics* 25, no. 2 (1963): 265–289.

Department of Justice. n.d. "Federal voting rights." https://www.justice.gov/crt/introduction-federal-voting-rights-laws-0.

Demillo, Andrew. 2018. "PAC won't pull ad suggesting 'lynching' if Democrats win." *The Spokesman-Review*. http://www.spokesman.com/stories/2018/oct/19/pac-wont-pull-ad-suggesting-lynching-if-Democrats-/.

Desposato, Scott W., and John R. Petrocik. "The variable incumbency advantage: New voters, redistricting, and the personal vote." *American Journal of Political Science* 47, no. 1 (2003): 18–32.

Dilger, Robert Jay. "Does politics matter? Partisanship's impact on state spending and taxes, 1985–95." *State and Local Government Review* 30, no. 2 (1998): 139–144.

Donnelly, Grace. 2018. "Georgia governor's race: 2018 candidate Michael Williams is campaigning on a 'deportation bus tour'." http://fortune.com/2018/05/16/georgia-governors-race-michael-williams/.

Douglas, Karen Manges, Rogelio Sáenz, and Aurelia Lorena Murga. "Immigration in the era of color-blind racism." *American Behavioral Scientist* 59, no. 11 (2015): 1429–1451.

Drucker, David M. 2018. "Why the blue wave is dying in the fight for the Senate." *New York Post*, October 20, 2018. https://nypost.com/2018/10/20/why-the-blue-wave-is-dying-in-the-fight-for-the-senate/.

Dutt, Pushan, and Mitra Devashish. "Political ideology and endogenous trade policy: An empirical investigation." *Review of Economics and Statistics* 87, no. 1 (2005): 59–72.

Dye, Thomas R. "Politics versus economics: The development of the literature on policy determination." *Policy Studies Journal* 7, no. 4 (1979): 652–662.

Edelson, Jack, Alexander Alduncin, Christopher Krewson, James A. Sieja, and Joseph E. Uscinski. "The effect of conspiratorial thinking and motivated reasoning on belief in election fraud." *Political Research Quarterly* 70, no. 4 (2017): 933–946.

Epstein, David, and Sharyn O'Halloran. "A strategic dominance argument for retaining section 5 of the VRA." *Election Law Journal* 5, no. 3 (2006): 283–292.

Erikson, Robert S., Gerald C. Wright, and John P. McIver. 1993. *Statehouse Democracy: Public Opinion and Policy in the American States.* Cambridge University Press.

Fair, Ray C. "The effect of economic events on votes for president: 1984 update." *Political Behavior* 10, no. 2 (1988): 168–179.

Fordham, Benjamin. "Partisanship, macroeconomic policy, and US uses of force, 1949–1994." *Journal of Conflict Resolution* 42, no. 4 (1998): 418–439.

Friedman, Adam. 2019. "Election commission won't change early voting times despite pleas from the community." *Jackson Sun*, March 12, 2019.

Garand, James C., and Rebecca M. Hendrick. "Expenditure tradeoffs in the American States: A longitudinal Test, 1948–1984." *Western Political Quarterly* 44, no. 4 (1991): 915–940.

Gawthrope, Andrew. 2018. "The midterms revealed the power of partisanship and whiteness." *The Guardian*, November 8, 2018. https://www.theguardian.com/commentisfree/2018/nov/08/midterms-Republicans-partisanship-white-identity-politics.

General Accounting Office. 1984. *Bilingual Voting Assistance Provided and Costs 1984 Report.* United States Government.

Gordon, Tracy. 2012. *State and Local Budgets and the Great Recession.* Washington, DC: The Brookings Institution.

Gomillion v. Lightfood 364 US 339 Supreme Court (1960).

Greenwald, Anthony G., Colin Tucker Smith, N. Sriram, Yoav Bar-Anan, and Brian A. Nosek. "Implicit race attitudes predicted vote in the 2008 US presidential election." *Analyses of Social Issues and Public Policy* 9, no. 1 (2009): 241–253.

Grofman, Bernard, and Arend Lijphart, eds. 1986. *Electoral Laws and Their Political Consequences.* Vol. 1. Algora Publishing.

Groseclose, Tim, and Nolan McCarty. "The politics of blame: Bargaining before an audience." *American Journal of Political Science* 45, no. 1 (2001): 100–119.

Gronke, Paul, William Hicks, Seth C. McKee, Charles Stewart III, and James Dunham. "Voter ID laws: A view from the public." (2015). MIT Political Science Department Research Paper No. 2015–13.

Guinn v. United States, 238 US 347 - Supreme Court (1915).

Hajnal, Zoltan, Nazita Lajevardi, and Lindsay Nielson. "Voter identification laws and the suppression of minority votes." *The Journal of Politics* 79, no. 2 (2017): 363–379.

Harvey, Alice E. "Ex-felon disenfranchisement and its influence on the black vote: The need for a second look." *University of Pennsylvania Law Review* 142 (1993): 1145.

Hancock, Jason. 2014. "Early-voting proposal in Missouri meets with skepticism." *The Kansas City Star*, October 14, 2014.

Hansford, Thomas G., and Brad T. Gomez. "Reevaluating the sociotropic economic voting hypothesis." *Electoral Studies* 39 (2015): 15–25.

Hawley, George. 2017. *Making Sense of the Alt Right*. Columbia University Press.

Hayes, Matthew, Matthew V. Hibbing, and Tracy Sulkin. "Redistricting, responsiveness, and issue attention." *Legislative Studies Quarterly* 35, no. 1 (2010): 91–115.

Henisz, Witold Jerzy. "Political institutions and policy volatility." *Economics & Politics* 16, no. 1 (2004): 1–27.

Herrman, John. 2016. "Donald Trump finds support in Reddit's unruly corners." *New York Times*, April 8. Retrieved from: www.nytimes.com/2016/04/09/business/media/in-reddits-unruly-corners-trump-finds-support.html.

Hibbing, John R., and Elizabeth Theiss-Morse. 1995. *Congress as Public Enemy: Public Attitudes toward American Political Institutions*. Boston, MA: Cambridge University Press.

Hibbing, John R., and Elizabeth Theiss-Morse. 2002. *Stealth Democracy: Americans' beliefs about How Government should Work*. Boston, MA: Cambridge University Press.

Hicks, William D., Seth C. McKee, and Daniel A. Smith. "The determinants of state legislator support for restrictive voter ID laws." *State Politics & Policy Quarterly* 16, no. 4 (2016): 411–431.

Hicks, William D., Seth C. McKee, Mitchell D. Sellers, and Daniel A. Smith. "A principle or a strategy? Voter identification laws and partisan competition in the American States." *Political Research Quarterly* 68, no. 1 (2015): 18–33.

Highton, Benjamin. "Easy registration and voter turnout." *The Journal of Politics* 59, no. 2 (1997): 565–575.

Highton, Benjamin. "Voter registration and turnout in the United States." *Perspectives on Politics* 2, no. 3 (2004): 507–515.

Hjalmarsson, Randi, and Mark Lopez. "The voting behavior of young disenfranchised felons: Would they vote if they could?" *American Law and Economics Review* 12, no. 2 (2010): 356–393.

Hochschild, Arlie Russell. 2018. *Strangers in their Own Land: Anger and Mourning on the American Right*. The New Press.

Howell, Ed. 2019. "Merrill: Early voting not needed in Alabama." *Daily Mountain Edge*, March 31, 2019.

Hudson, Jerome. 2011. "Democrats should know Jim crow, they created him." *Human Events*. http://humanevents.com/2011/07/10/Democrats-should-know-jim-crow-they-created-him/.

Huber, Gregory A., and Thomas J. Espenshade. "Neo-isolationism, balanced-budget conservatism, and the fiscal impacts of immigrants." *International Migration Review* 31, no. 4 (1997): 1031–1054.

Howard, Hunter. 2019. Mapped using QGIS 3.10 and Windows 10. State datasets retrieved from the National Atlas of the United States, 1:1,000,000-Scale datasets March 2016, 2nd edition. Identification law data obtained from ncsl.org.

Hwang, Sung-Don, and Virginia Gray. "External limits and internal determinants of state public policy." *Western Political Quarterly* 44, no. 2 (1991): 277–298.

Jacobs, David, and Daniel Tope. "The politics of resentment in the post–civil rights era: Minority threat, homicide, and ideological voting in congress." *American Journal of Sociology* 112, no. 5 (2007): 1458–1494.

Jacobson, Gary C. "Strategic politicians and the dynamics of US House elections, 1946–86." *American Political Science Review* 83, no. 3 (1989): 773–793.

Jones, Bradley. 2016. "Americans' views of immigrants marked by widening partisan, generational divides." *Pew Research Center Fact Tank*, April 15. Retrieved from: www.pewresearch.org/fact-tank/2016/04/15/americans-views-of-immigrants-marked-by-widening-partisan-generational-divides/.

Kellogg, Sarah. "Voter ID laws: Partisan electioneering or good government." *Washington Lawyer* 27 (2012): 23.

Kimball, David C., Martha Kropf, and Lindsay Battles. "Helping America vote? Election administration, partisanship, and provisional voting in the 2004 election." *Election Law Journal* 5, no. 4 (2006): 447–461.

Kinder, Donald R., and D. Roderick Kiewiet. "Sociotropic politics: The American case." *British Journal of Political Science* 11, no. 2 (1981): 129–161.

Kinder, Donald R., and David O. Sears. "Prejudice and politics: Symbolic racism versus racial threats to the good life." *Journal of Personality and Social Psychology* 40, no. 3 (1981): 414.

Knack, Stephen, and James White. "Election-day registration and turnout inequality." *Political Behavior* 22, no. 1 (2000): 29–44.

Krehbiel, Keith. "Where's the party?" *British Journal of Political Science* 23, no. 2 (1993): 235–266.

Krehbiel, Keith. 1998. *Pivotal Politics: A Theory of US Lawmaking*. Chicago, IL: University of Chicago Press.

Lee, Brian. 2018. "Local clerks prepare for early voting, which starts Monday." *The Telegram*. https://www.telegram.com/news/20181020/local-clerks-prepare-for-early-voting-which-starts-monday.

Lee, Frances E. 2009. *Beyond Ideology: Politics, Principles, and Partisanship in the US Senate*. University of Chicago Press.

LeVine, Robert A., and Donald T. Campbell. 1972. *Ethnocentrism: Theories of Conflict, Ethnic Attitudes, and Group Behavior*. John Wiley and Sons.

Lewis-Beck, Michael S. "The relative importance of socioeconomic and political variables for public policy." *American Political Science Review* 71, no. 2 (1977): 559–566.

Lowry, Rich. 2014. "The poll tax that wasn't." *Politico*, October 22.

Lublin, D.I. "Quality, not quantity: Strategic politicians in US Senate elections, 1952–1990." *The Journal of Politics* 56, no. 1 (1994): 228–241.

Lublin, David, and D. Stephen Voss. "Racial redistricting and realignment in Southern state legislatures." *American Journal of Political Science* 44, no. 4 (2000): 792–810.

Madani, Doha. 2019. "Civil rights groups sue Florida over 'poll tax' aw to restore felon voters rights." *NBC News*, June 28, 2019.

Major, Brenda, Alison Blodorn, and Gregory Major Blascovich. "The threat of increasing diversity: Why many White Americans support Trump in the 2016 presidential election." *Group Processes & Intergroup Relations* 21, no .6 (2016): 931–940.

Manza, Jeff, Clem Brooks, and Christopher Uggen. "Public attitudes toward felon disenfranchisement in the United States." *Public Opinion Quarterly* 68, no. 2 (2004): 275–286.

Manza, Jeff, and Christopher Uggen. 2008. *Locked Out: Felon Disenfranchisement and American Democracy*. Oxford University Press.

Marquette, Jesse F., and Katherine A. Hinckley. "Competition, control and spurious covariation: A longitudinal analysis of state spending." *American Journal of Political Science* 25, no. 2 (1981): 362–375.

Maxwell, Angie, and T. Wayne Parent. "The Obama trigger: Presidential approval and Tea Party membership." *Social Science Quarterly* 93, no. 5 (2012): 1384–1401.

McKee, Seth C. "The effects of redistricting on voting behavior in incumbent US House elections, 1992—1994." *Political Research Quarterly* 61, no. 1 (2008): 122–133.

McKee, Seth C. "Politics is local: State legislator voting on restrictive voter identification legislation." *Research & Politics* 2, no. 3 (2015): 2053168015589804.

McKenzie, Mark Jonathan. "The influence of partisanship, ideology, and the law on redistricting decisions in the federal courts." *Political Research Quarterly* 65, no. 4 (2012): 799–813.

McGettigan, Timothy. 2016. "Donald Trump and White Racism" (August 15, 2016). Available at SSRN: https://ssrn.com/abstract=2823974.

Meredith, Marc, and Michael Morse. "The politics of the restoration of ex-felon voting rights: The case of Iowa." *Quarterly Journal of Political Science* 10, no. 1 (2015): 41–100.

Milner, Helen V., and Benjamin Judkins. "Partisanship, trade policy, and globalization: Is there a left–right divide on trade policy?" *International Studies Quarterly* 48, no. 1 (2004): 95–119.

Mukherjee, Roopali. "Antiracism limited: A pre-history of post-race." *Cultural Studies* 30, no. 1 (2016): 47–77.

Nadeau, R., and M.S. Lewis-Beck. "National economic voting in US presidential elections." *Journal of Politics* 63, no. 1 (2001): 159–181.

National Endowment for the Humanities (NEH). 2014. "Reconstruction vs. redemption." https://www.neh.gov/news/reconstruction-vs-redemption.

National Council of State Legislatures (NCSL). 2019. "State partisan composition." http://www.ncsl.org/research/about-state-legislatures/partisan-composition.aspx.

National Conference of State Legislatures (NCSL). 2018a. "Election costs: What states pay." August 3, 2018. http://www.ncsl.org/research/elections-and-campaigns/election-costs.aspx.

National Conference of State Legislatures (NCSL). 2018b. "The price of democracy: Splitting the bill for elections." http://www.ncsl.org/research/elections-and-campaigns/the-price-of-democracy-splitting-the-bill-for-elections.aspx.

National Latino Leadership Agenda. 2015. "NHLA supports Univision decision to cut ties with Trump, urges NBCU to the same." June 27.

National Public Radio (NPR). 2013. "The racial history of the grandfather clause." https://www.npr.org/sections/codeswitch/2013/10/21/239081586/the-racial-history-of-the-grandfather-clause.

Neely, G. W., and L. E. Richardson Jr. "Who is early voting? An individual level examination." *The Social Science Journal* 38 (2001): 381–392.

Niemi, Richard G., and Alan I. Abramowitz. "Partisan redistricting and the 1992 congressional elections." *The Journal of Politics* 56, no. 3 (1994): 811–817.

Niemi, Richard G., Bernard Grofman, Carl Carlucci, and Thomas Hofeller. "Measuring compactness and the role of a compactness standard in a test for partisan and racial gerrymandering." *The Journal of Politics* 52, no. 4 (1990): 1155–1181.

Niemi, Richard G., and Laura R. Winsky. "The persistence of partisan redistricting effects in congressional elections in the 1970s and 1980s." *The Journal of Politics* 54, no. 2 (1992): 565–572.

O'Reilly, Kenneth. "The Jim crow policies of Woodrow Wilson." *The Journal of Blacks in Higher Education*, no. 17 (1997): 117–121.

Obergefell v. Hodges, 135 S. Ct. 2071 – 2015.

Oliff, Phil, Chris Mai, and Vincent Palacios. 2012. *States Continue to Feel Recession's Impact.* Washington, DC: Center on Budget and Policy Priorities. Available at: http://www. cbpp.org/cms/index.cfm?fa=view&id=711.

Overby, L. Marvin, and Kenneth M. Cosgrove. "Unintended consequences? Racial redistricting and the representation of minority interests." *The Journal of Politics* 58, no. 2 (1996): 540–550.

Pew Center on the States. 2012. *The Widening Gap Update.* Washington, DC: Pew Center on the States. Available at: http://www.pewstates. org/research/reports/the-widening-gap-update- 85899398241.

Peterson, Paul E., and Mark C. Rom. 1990. *Welfare Magnets: A Case for a National Welfare Standard.* Washington, DC: The Brookings Institution.

Petrocik, John R. "Issue ownership in presidential elections, with a 1980 case study." *American Journal of Political Science* 40, no. 3 (1996): 825–850.

Plotnick, Robert D., and Richard F. Winters. "Party, political liberalism, and redistribution: An application to the American states." *American Politics Quarterly* 18, no. 4 (1990): 430–458.

Poterba, James M. "State responses to fiscal crises: The effects of budgetary institutions and politics." *Journal of political Economy* 102, no. 4 (1994): 799–821.

Reilly, Shauna. 2015. *Language Assistance under the Voting Rights Act.* Lanham, MD: Lexington Press.

Reynolds v. Sims 377 US 533 Supreme Court (1964).

Riser, R. Volney. 2010. *Defying Disfranchisement: Black Voting Rights Activism in the Jim Crow South, 1890–1908.* Baton Rouge: Louisiana State University Press.

Rocha, Rene R., and Tetsuya Matsubayashi. "The politics of race and voter ID laws in the states: The return of Jim Crow?" *Political Research Quarterly* 67, no. 3 (2014): 666–679.

Roe v. Wade, 410 U.S. 113 (1973).

RUCHO v. Common Cause, 2019.

Rueben, Kim, Megan Randall, and Aravind Boddupalli. 2018. "Budget processes and the great recession: How state fiscal institutions shape tax and spending decisions." *Urban Institute Report.*

Rush, Mark E. *Does Redistricting Make a Difference?: Partisan Representation and Electoral Behavior.* Lanham, MD: Lexington Books, 2000.

Schaffner, Brian F., Michael W. Wagner, and Jonathan Winburn. "Incumbents out, party in? Term limits and partisan redistricting in state legislatures." *State Politics & Policy Quarterly* 4, no. 4 (2004): 396–414.

Skocpol, Theda, and Vanessa Williamson. 2016. *The Tea Party and the Remaking of Republican Conservatism.* Oxford University Press.

Sharpe, Christine Leveaux, and James C. Garand. "Race, roll calls, and redistricting: The impact of race-based redistricting on congressional roll-call." *Political Research Quarterly* 54, no. 1 (2001): 31–51.

Shaw v. Reno, 509 US 630 – 1993.

Shepherd, N. Jay. "Abridge too far: Racial gerrymandering, the fifteenth amendment, and Shaw v. Reno." *Boston College Third World Law Journal* 14 (1994): 337.

Sieger, Edward. 2014. "County officials remain opposed to New Jersey early voting bill." *The Express-Times,* February 10, 2014. https://www.lehighvalleylive.com/br eaking-news/2014/02/new_jersey_senate_considering.html.

Silberstein, Rachel. 2019. "Legislature passes sweeping electoral reforms." *Times Union,* January 18, 2019.

Silver, Nate. 2018. "How FiveThirtyEight's 2018 midterm forecast did." December 4, 2018. https://fivethirtyeight.com/features/how-fivethirtyeights-2018-midterm -forecasts-did/.

Simmons, Randy T., Diana W. Thomas, and Ryan M. Yonk. "Bootleggers, Baptists, and political entrepreneurs: key players in the rational game and morality play of regulatory politics." *The Independent Review* 15, no. 3 (2011): 367–381.

Sinclair-Chapman, Valeria, and Melanye Price. "Black politics, the 2008 election, and the (im) possibility of race transcendence." *PS: Political Science & Politics* 41, no. 4 (2008): 739–745.

Sobel, Richard, and Robert Ellis Smith. "Voter-ID laws discourage participation, particularly among minorities, and trigger a constitutional remedy in lost representation." *PS: Political Science & Politics* 42, no. 1 (2009): 107–110.

Smith, Timothy. 2019. "How republicans stopped worrying about the right to vote." *Talking Points Memo,* June 20, 2019. https://talkingpointsmemo.com/cafe/Repub lican-decade-voter-suppression-efforts.

Smith v. Allwright, 321 U.S. 649 (1944).

Stein, Robert M. "Economic voting for governor and US senator: The electoral consequences of federalism." *The Journal of Politics* 52, no. 1 (1990): 29–53.

Stephan, W. G., O. Ybarra, and G. Bachman. "Prejudice toward immigrants." *Journal of Applied Social Psychology* 29, no. 11 (1999): 2221–2237.

Stewart, Emily. 2018. "The Battle over early voting, explained: Making voting more convenient is surprisingly controversial." *Vox.com,* November 4, 2018.

Squire, Peverill. "Results of partisan redistricting in seven US states during the 1970s." *Legislative Studies Quarterly* 10, no. 2 (1985): 259–266.

Squire, Peverill. "The partisan consequences of congressional redistricting." *American Politics Quarterly* 23, no. 2 (1995): 229–240.

Subtirelu, Nicholas Close. "Donald Trump supporters and the denial of racism." *Journal of Language Aggression and Conflict* 5, no. 2 (2017): 323–346.

Sullivan, Sean, and David Weigel. 2015. "Some republican hopefuls criticize Trump's Muslim 'shutdown' call more strongly than others." *Washington Post*, December 7. Retrieved from: https://www.washingtonpost.com/news/post-politics/wp/2015/12/07/some-Republican-hopefuls-criticize-trumps-muslim-shutdown-call-more-strongly-than-others/.

Teasley, Martell, and David Ikard. "Barack Obama and the politics of race: The myth of postracism in America." *Journal of Black Studies* 40, no. 3 (2010): 411–425.

Terry v. Adams 345 US 461 Supreme Court (1953).

The Guardian. 2018. "Is this the most racist US midterms campaign ever?" *The Guardian*. https://www.theguardian.com/us-news/2018/nov/04/us-midterms-2018-trump-racist-attack-ads-Republicans.

Tolbert, Caroline J., and John A. Grummel. "Revisiting the racial threat hypothesis: White voter support for California's Proposition 209." *State Politics & Policy Quarterly* (2003): 183–202.

Uggen, Christopher, and Jeff Manza. "Democratic contraction? Political consequences of felon disenfranchisement in the United States." *American Sociological Review* 67, no. 6 (2002): 777–803.

Uggen, Christopher, Jeff Manza, and Melissa Thompson. "Citizenship, democracy, and the civic reintegration of criminal offenders." *The Annals of the American Academy of Political and Social Science* 605, no. 1 (2006): 281–310.

U.S. Bureau of the Census. 2011. *Annual Survey of State and Local Government Finances*. Washington, DC, 2011.

U.S. Government Accountability Office. April 2011. *State and Local Governments' Fiscal Outlook*. Washington, DC.

US Census. 2018a. "Annual survey of state government finances." https://www.census.gov/programs-surveys/gov-finances.html

US Census. 2018b. https://www.census.gov/data/datasets/time-series/demo/popest/intercensal-2000-2010-state.html.

US Census. 2017. "American community survey." https://www.census.gov/programs-surveys/acs.

US Census. 2010. "Population and housing unit counts." https://www.census.gov/prod/cen2010/cph-2-1.pdf.

US Census Bureau Geography Program. n.d. "Census regions and divisions of the United States." https://www2.census.gov/geo/pdfs/maps-data/maps/reference/us_regdiv.pdf.

US Election Assistance Commission. 2019. "Election and administration voting survey." https://www.eac.gov/research-and-data/datasets-codebooks-and-surveys/.

U.S. Government Accountability Office. *State and Local Governments' Fiscal Outlook*. Washington, DC, April 2012. Available at: http:// www.gao.gov/products/GAO-12-523SP.

Voting Rights Institute. 2015. "The real costs of voter ID laws." Voting Rights Institute. http://assets.Democrats.org/pdfs/photoid/Dems-report-real_cost_of_voting_ID.pdf.

Waymer, Damion, and Robert L. Heath. "Black voter dilution, American exceptionalism, and racial gerrymandering: The paradox of the positive in political public relations." *Journal of Black Studies* 47, no. 7 (2016): 635–658.

Weiser, Wendy R. "How much of a difference did new voting restrictions make in yesterday's close races?" *Brennan Center for Justice at New York University School of Law* (2014).

Wesberry v. Sanders 361 US 1 Supreme Court (1964).

Wilson, David C., and Paul R. Brewer. "The foundations of public opinion on voter ID laws: Political predispositions, racial resentment, and information effects." *Public Opinion Quarterly* 77, no. 4 (2013): 962–984.

Wilson, David C., Paul R. Brewer, and Phoebe Theodora Rosenbluth. "Racial imagery and support for voter ID laws." *Race and Social Problems* 6, no. 4 (2014): 365–371.

Wingfield, Adia Harvey, and Joe Feagin. "The racial dialectic: President Barack Obama and the white racial frame." *Qualitative Sociology* 35, no. 2 (2012): 143–162.

Wolf, Stephen. "Race Ipsa: Vote dilution, racial gerrymandering, and the presumption of racial discrimination." *Notre Dame Journal of Legal Ethics & Public Policy* 11 (1997): 225.

Wormser, Richard. n.d. "Rise and Fall of Jim Crow." PBS. https://www.thirteen.org/wnet/jimcrow/stories_events_reconstruct.html.

Yandle, Bruce. "Bootleggers and Baptists-the education of a regulatory economists." *Regulation* 7 (1983): 12.

Index

About the Author

Dr. Shauna Reilly is Professor of Political Science and Director for the Institute for Student Research and Creative Activity at Northern Kentucky University. She has written extensively on electoral access and barriers to participation.

www.ingramcontent.com/pod-product-compliance
Lightning Source LLC
Chambersburg PA
CBHW022323280326
41932CB00010B/1205